T0194058

ON THE
SHELF

WAITING ON GOD'S DIRECTIONS

JAMES E. BROOKS

WESTBOW
PRESS®
A DIVISION OF THOMAS NELSON
& ZONDERVAN

Copyright © 2018 James E. Brooks.

All rights reserved. No part of this book may be used or reproduced by any means, graphic, electronic, or mechanical, including photocopying, recording, taping or by any information storage retrieval system without the written permission of the author except in the case of brief quotations embodied in critical articles and reviews.

Scripture taken from the King James Version of the Bible.

WestBow Press books may be ordered through booksellers or by contacting:

WestBow Press
A Division of Thomas Nelson & Zondervan
1663 Liberty Drive
Bloomington, IN 47403
www.westbowpress.com
1 (866) 928-1240

Because of the dynamic nature of the Internet, any web addresses or links contained in this book may have changed since publication and may no longer be valid. The views expressed in this work are solely those of the author and do not necessarily reflect the views of the publisher, and the publisher hereby disclaims any responsibility for them.

Any people depicted in stock imagery provided by Getty Images are models, and such images are being used for illustrative purposes only. Certain stock imagery © Getty Images.

ISBN: 978-1-9736-2002-0 (sc)
ISBN: 978-1-9736-2001-3 (e)

Library of Congress Control Number: 2018901846

Print information available on the last page.

WestBow Press rev. date: 03/13/2018

To my wife, Patty, who experienced everything I did and encouraged me to finish this book.

CHAPTER 1

I am finally going to finish writing this book I began years ago. I feel it is time to put to work some of the wisdom and the experience God has put into my life through this journey. Having passed through spiritual dimensions that have helped shape and prepare me, I am far from being an authority on the subject of waiting on God. I am the least of those who understand these things, and for this cause, I have put off writing for a long time. Part of the reason I hesitated so long is because I am still living what needs to be written, and part of it is my insecurity about such matters. Writing about the personal and private events in my life is sometimes joyful and sometimes not so joyful. My life seems to be a continuous, swirling saga of being on and off of God's shelf. Please forgive me for the excessive use of personal references, but I have lived on the shelf. This shelf has become a familiar friend, a place of refuge, and a sanctuary of peace. If you find yourself on this shelf, it could be because you too are living in a place of isolation and loneliness, without a glimmer of understanding. My prayer for you is that a flicker of direction and hope in the God who has a plan for your life will be renewed. I will have succeeded in my endeavor if you are blessed by something I share as we journey together through the pages of *On the Shelf*.

Feeling the loneliness of separation from the mainstream of activities when God places your life on hold gives special meaning to this scripture: "And he took him aside from the multitude" (Mark 7:33).

You might also be the kind of person who is able to take the worst kind of stress and strain along with intense suffering yet fall to pieces completely when you are sidetracked or put on the shelf from all of your normal spiritual activities. When you are forced into some form of isolation, by your own choosing or by the hand of others, God can and will meet with you there and begin a new direction in your ministry and life. Yes, He will. The preparation of education and familiarization with new and different tactics and practices in the kingdom of God usually begin when you are on this shelf. Will you submit to Him?

> For thus saith the high and lofty One that inhabiteth eternity, whose name is Holy; I dwell in the high and holy place, with him also that is of a contrite and humble spirit, to revive the spirit of the humble, and to revive the heart of the contrite ones. (Isaiah 57:15)

God has a plan.

In the beginning, *On the Shelf* was inspired by a situation I found myself in when I resigned from my pastorate and began attending another church while waiting on the Lord to provide me with new direction and open doors of opportunity. The pastor of the church I was visiting this particular day preached a sermon that spoke about the spiritual situation of a person who was in the hands of the Master Potter. He mentioned the potter's house from the book of the prophet Jeremiah. These five points—the clay, the potter's wheel, the vessel the potter desired to produce, the fire in the kiln, and finally, the finished product—rounded out his sermon that Sunday morning. He spoke about a shelf that the clay had been placed on while waiting for the potter to choose its form. I imagined it to be a shelf much like the one that my own life sat upon. It was a dark, lonely, and sometimes fearful place that now had become just a waiting and wondering process of what God would choose for me if I were a lump of pottery clay. The scripture came to me that day from the book of Isaiah. "But now, O LORD, thou art our father; we are the clay, and thou our potter; and we all are the work of thy hand" (Isaiah 64:8).

As ministers and ministry workers, we sometimes find times in our lives when we are "shelved" by the Lord. We feel abandoned, unfulfilled, and picked over—until that sacred moment when the great potter reaches toward the shelf and chooses us. I have been living this moment, sitting on a shelf of waiting and praying for the will of God and the open door of opportunity in my ministry many times. Perhaps others may be inspired by my failures and victories and will decide they also must hang on a little longer with a renewed hope. I hope you will. The results can be exciting and fulfilling.

The Broken Sword

This I beheld, or dreamed it in a dream: There spread a cloud of dust along a plain;
And underneath the cloud, or in it, raged a furious battle, and men yelled, and swords
Shocked upon swords and shields. A prince's banner Wavered, then staggered backward, hemmed by foes.
A craven hung along the battles edge, And thought, "Had I a sword of keener steel—That blue blade that the king's son bears—but this Blunt thing—! He snapt and flung it from his hand, And lowering crept away and left the field. Then came the king's son, wounded, sore bestead And weaponless, and saw the broken sword, Hilt-buried in the dry and trodden sand. And ran and snatched it, and with battle shout Lifted afresh, he hewed his enemy down, And saved a great cause that heroic day. (William L. Stidger, based on Psalm 31:12)

I first read this poem quickly and nearly missed the very point the author was making. After the third attempt at reading, I think I grasped the meaning and found the sword that was thought to be a blessing. I found in this poem that even a broken, rejected sword can become a weapon of importance in the hand of a skilled, determined hand of passion. I believe that in a life that has been shelved and pushed into the obscurity of the place of waiting, that skilled hand is the hand of Jesus.

Let Jesus take you in His hand one more time and win battles you never thought possible. Psalm 31:12 says, "I am forgotten as a dead man out of mind: I am like a broken vessel." Ministers are like vessels that can perish, break, and become irreparable and useless without the guidance of God's input, and this is a miserable existence indeed. A vessel that is supposed to be a special vessel that has been called by the Holy Spirit and set apart or sanctified for His special use is now relegated to the loneliness of the desert experience. What is going on? Where are my close friends and mentors now when I need them the most?

The mind can play mean tricks with feelings of loneliness while in between appointments of positions of service. Depression is only a step away sometimes. I know not everyone travels this path, but some of us do. Such is the state of a man forsaken by those he has been friends with for many years. Now that he is broken, they leave him because he is not as useful to them, and they find no common ground of experience with him as a broken vessel. Now he is feared by those who are not sidelined by such conditions, and he is often avoided because they don't know what to do or what to say. But the greatest gift any one friend can give to someone who is being shelved and between appointments is the gift I call the *gift of presence*. Just show up, and be there. The gift of presence is the most expensive gift in the world.

"Useless" may be too harsh a description, but when you are on the up-and-up and everything is going great, the friends you find may be fair-weather friends. They are only there in the good times, but when the going gets rough, they have other, rather serious duties that command their time and must be attended to urgently. The true friends are usually counted in the singular and rarely are more than two. True friends, who love you when the going is great *and* when the going is rough, still love you and stick closer than a brother to you; true friends are rare and precious. Oh Lord, give me friends that stay closer than a brother. This could be the story of a man who has been placed on the shelf of God's intentions. But one day the plan God has had all along brings him out from the desert and God begins to use him in miraculous ways. The Lord begins to prepare him for a particular outcome. Like clay that has been placed on purpose on the shelf until it is ready to be used on the wheel to prepare it for a new design and a new purpose, it waits.

"Needing a friend to help me in the end, where could I go but to the Lord?" This is part of an old song we sang during congregational worship when I was a boy. Where do the pastors go when they need counsel? Who counsels the counselors? Where do the ministers go when they need spiritual direction? Some would love to have a place of refuge for the weary, worried, and wondering ministers who are in this condition. Is there such a safe place to unburden heavy hearts and clouded minds? Does God have a place where the weary and worried servant of God can recuperate in a stress-free environment? Yes, there is.

A wise man once said that a dull axe requires more strength to cut the wood than a sharp one. So a time of sharpening the axe may be in order. Are you at this place? Yes, Jesus said, "Come unto me, all ye that are burdened and heavy laden and I will give you rest" (Matthew 11:28). Sometimes life leaves you dangling with the thought *Where could I go but to the Lord?* Being on the shelf brings you before the throne of the Almighty. At least the opportunity to seek His counsel is made available in the solitude this shelf experience provides. It is a great time for seeking the counsel of God's wisdom in prayer and through the scripture. But too often we waste the opportunity God has handed us for meditation, and finding ourselves alone, we think we are being mistreated. Faith and trust in God kept Moses during the long years of leading a stubborn and rebellious people in the wilderness. He needed the guiding hand of God and a prayer meeting many times to keep the Israelites following the direction of the cloud by day and the fire by night. Maybe they only followed with their feet for the first forty years, but the next forty years, their soul and spirit caught up in time to make the Jordan River crossing with Joshua.

Just a little talk with Jesus can often give us directions in our situations when we are without direction. Sometimes withdrawing from the public forum provides a place of solitude and loneliness. Separating from the crowds can be a solution for stress and overloaded nerves. The God-designed shelf becomes a prime place of recovery. Being on the shelf isn't a solitary confinement but a refocusing of the importance of obeying the direction of God's finger that points in the right direction. When every door is closed, and there are no helping hands in sight, we sit in silence, wondering and waiting. Having no place to unburden the heavy load and no one to guide our steps, the deserted feeling you experience may be the shelf that will become your refuge and healing and not a place of solitary confinement. Counseled by faith, the trust you place in Jesus Christ at first may not seem to be perfect or complete. Just the size of a mustard seed, but that small faith can do wonders. It is usually a prayer that is wavering, trembling, fearful, and weak that approaches the presence of God. His faith created the world and all that is in it. It started with Genesis 1:1 and will end with Genesis 1:1. In the beginning, God and in the end it will be just God. You will gradually grow in faith as the trial you are in progresses, and finally you will be able to resume your normal duties and activities.

Stay faithful. Put your trust in His trust. There will come a day when the waiting is over, the shelf life will be replaced with a purpose, and you will arise and go forth victorious. So is there a need for faith when a person has been sidelined and temporarily out of the loop of full time ministry? Yes. Put your trust in Jesus. Eventually you will emerge into the light again. Just stay faithful, be patient, and wait on Him. He will bring you out. More than once did my very dear friend Rev. T. W. Barnes personally tell me,

> Boy, when the Lord filled you with His Spirit, He put everything you would need from that day on in that infilling of the Spirit. You've got everything you need for the journey already. The great oak tree didn't ask what to do when it was growing and the seasons were changing. It didn't wonder what was happening to it. No, it was already programmed into that acorn what to do. So the Holy Spirit will teach you everything you need to know. You just have to listen to Him.

The apostle James says that faith and wisdom are companions.

> If any of you lack wisdom, let him ask of God, that giveth to all men liberally, and upbraideth not; and it shall be given him. But let him ask in faith, nothing wavering. For he that wavereth is like a wave of the sea driven with the wind and tossed. For let not that man think that he shall receive any thing of the Lord. A double minded man is unstable in all his ways. (James 1:5–8)

God's Word says in Hebrews 11:1 that "faith is the substance of things hoped for." And Ecclesiastes 1:18 tells us, "For in much wisdom is much grief: and he that increaseth knowledge increaseth sorrow." This scripture imparts to us that the more we know of ourselves, the less satisfied we are with our own hearts. Sitting on a shelf in the dark of not understanding why, and the cold feeling of what has happened to you, is a hard pill to swallow. Sometimes a little light begins to pierce your darkness with the understanding that God is really after a worshipper to worship Him and not necessarily after a worker to correct Him. Allow God's will to be performed, and the results will somehow line your expectations up with His plan.

True happiness comes from faith and communion with God, so how do these two powerful frames of mind shape our futures? With that faith that produces the fear of the Lord, you also get understanding. God is no respecter of persons, and He will bless the genuine believer with the understanding that can make all the difference in the world. With this communication you have with God, your faith then is the counsel that the counselors turn to and search for in times of testing. Not to one another? Not always. You see, the arm of flesh will fail you, but God's Word will refresh, encourage, and direct you. When we carry one another's burden, we are fulfilling the command to be a keeper of our brother's interests. The answer lies within you. Search your heart and soul, and the rewarder of those who sincerely seek understanding will see to it that you find it.

You cannot show faith without works, hope without works, or love without works. For faith without works isn't faith. It is doubt. And hope without works isn't hope. It is hopelessness. So then love without works isn't love. It is hypocrisy. Then faith is the direct contact with the supernatural world that supplies all your needs according to His riches in glory. Sometimes even the faithful fail God in this dimension. The shelf can teach you many things. Necessity is not only the mother of invention; necessity is also the brother to innovation. So we sit up and pay close attention to our teacher called experience. She usually only needs to show us once. Sitting on a lonely shelf, we have our senses sharpened, you might say, by the experience that is swirling all around us. When the Piped Piper of experience pipes, it seems we listen carefully and usually follow where it leads.

Abram became the Father of the Faithful, but long before he was known as a friend of God, he was known to Pharaoh in Genesis 7 as an unfaithful man to his wife, Sarah. Abraham said Sarah was his sister when she was actually his wife. God tests His men with tests of courage and trial. The shelf experience tested the courage in my life several times. Perhaps you are being tested right now. Above all, be honest with yourself and with your God. He knows your heart better than you know yourself. Stay faithful, remain calm, and wait on the Lord. He really does renew the strength. Keep your eyes on Him. He is watching you. If He sees a sparrow that falls, He sees you. There is an all-seeing eye watching you.

God will not change, but people will and do. God is not a man that He should change, but man must. Placing your faith in God's ultimate knowledge and abilities for your life will soothe and ease even the most troubled feelings of depressing thoughts and heartaches. Your time on the shelf can be a revelation, not destruction. Trust me: I've been there and will probably end up there again someday. Trusting your feelings results in oppression, and this leads to depression. These two feelings can lead you away from the peace that passes all understanding. So sit down at His feet and listen. He may be trying to tell you something. Hear the heartbeat of Jesus as the beloved disciple did. John was close enough to hear the heartbeat of Jesus as he leaned on Him at the Last Supper. Are you that close?

Counsel me, oh God. Speak to me *faith*. Sustain me; uphold me with Thy righteous counsel. I thought, *Now that's a switch.* I remember when a loved one was hospitalized and on the day of their scheduled surgery, I met a fellow minister in the hall outside of the waiting room. I guess he read the worry in my face so he took me aside to speak a kind and comforting word. "There's no need to worry," he began.

"Everything will be all right." I looked at him and asked, "Brother, I know it will be all right, but right now I need to know: where do pastors go when they need a pastor? Can you tell me?" He looked at me with a puzzled look on his face and said, "You know, I've been wondering that very thought." So where does the individual go if we are all sitting on a bench in the potter's room while waiting for action? We wait, wait, and wait. We wait until God chooses to lift us up. That's what we must do. And thank the Lord, we're not all on the shelf at the same time.

Here is where the question gets answered to those on the shelf. To the minister whose ministry is at a standstill, or seemingly over with, restore your relationship to God through prayer. To the ministry worker who has no hope of work in sight, rebuild that altar of prayer. To the missions person who feels abandoned and forgotten, there is an all-seeing eye, and you will go back to that first love and pray until heaven comes down and glory floods your soul again.

Nothing more and nothing less will supply the longing in your heart like stop, drop, and pray. Sounds too simple, doesn't it? It's true. Prayer will renew your communication with God. Get down on your knees or sit in a chair and pray. If you are in a bed, close your eyes and say, "Lord, here I am to worship." You don't need to get in a stained-glass voice to pray. Just a normal talking voice will do. We go to the Lord, and we stay there until He is through teaching us the simple truth of trust. Where do the counselors go when they need counseling? They had better go pray. I think I know a little bit more now than I did then, and after running around in circles, I finally ended up going to the Master. Oh, how I love Jesus!

He sends us to the backside of deserts, on shelves at the potter's house, and onto lonely islands of isolation. Sometimes it's a small city far removed from family, bright lights, and active involvement in anything except what is right before us. But sometimes from there the view can be breathtaking, if we'd only look up. Wait patiently on the Lord, obey Him, and let Him take care of the consequences. Focus on the answer, not the situation and circumstances. Circumstances control all things, but God controls the circumstances.

I once felt the need to be active in some capacity in a ministerial surrounding, and that was several years back. It was somewhere during an absence of spiritual direction in a time of life when there was a natural need for activity. I guess it was created by my constant involvement in the ministry. I had been involved in everything my spare time allowed, and now I was without purpose and direction like a ship without a sail. I was just drifting along with any breeze that blew, and I hoped I was going in the direction I wanted. I just didn't know how not to be involved in the pulpit ministry or any other ministry for that matter.

I think this simple example explains the feeling of the need to be busy doing. The old horse had pulled the milk wagon, day after day and year after year, and was finally let out to pasture and retired. He would never be required to pull the wagon again. But the following morning after he had been relieved from his duties, the milkman found the old horse waiting for him at the barn, standing between the traces of the wagon, ready to be hitched up. He just didn't know how not to go to work. Preachers are sometimes like that. We don't really know how not to be engaged in ministerial duties after we have left a church. It's just nature. Sometimes, a man of God hasn't yet found his niche in the ministry and is simply waiting for an open door. Sometimes God has a valley of education for him to pass through. Perhaps God is about to reeducate him with a shelf ministry. Then it's "shelf time."

Once I was waiting on new directions from the Lord to be confirmed, I was attending the church of a friend who gave me a bit of advice right when it felt like I couldn't take any more waiting for an answer from the Lord. He advised me, "Just show up for the services. Stay faithful.

Don't stay isolated long. Absorb the atmosphere of the services. And in due time, you will feel like participating again." I did. It did. And today I am so thankful for that helpful advice. Still I needed to hear the call, feel the anointing, and know that God had a specific place for me to labor in. You will too, my friend. You will also hear that call again. He has a still, soft voice.

During this time of sitting on the shelf and feeling that I had no direction, I felt cut off from my normal pastoral activities. And as I was spending my time in prayer, fasting, and studying the Word, I was reassured of the divine hand of direction in my life. Awaiting this next calling in the ministry, I experienced an unusual dream. I was standing at the railing of a ship at sea while looking toward the land. I saw the waters disappear. The floor of the sea was exposed, as if the tide had changed and suddenly gone out, leaving behind what had always been there but had been hidden from view. It now was fully exposed. I saw from the ship four or five bright-red, shiny rocks. These were barely visible in the mud, but the light had revealed them to me. I quickly went after these stones. So many fellow passengers along the railing of the ship attempted to dissuade me from such a dangerous endeavor. When I stepped off the ship onto the muddy ocean floor, I fully expected to sink into the mud. But contrary to the frantic advice of those on board who were fearful for me, I did not sink. Picking up these red, shiny objects, I realized that they were rubies of great value. They were each of a different shape and size. I really believed the tide had turned for my ministry. Several weeks later, I was in the middle of a revival that promised to bring souls into the "old ship of Zion."

Will you be willing to submit cheerfully to the pressure of the Master's hand as your life is being shaped on the wheel or left sitting in the dark, damp storage? I believe we have been promised—or at least been made aware of—things that now are hidden, but they are about to be revealed to you. "They that wait upon the Lord ..." (Isaiah 40:31). Here you sit on the shelf in the potter's house while valuable treasures of people are waiting on you to rescue them, right? Everywhere are souls lying beneath the murky waters of this life, waiting for the tide to turn in their lives and waiting for someone to pick them up, to bring value to them and to the church. You are that man or woman, right?

Wisdom, instruction, and understanding will be your guide as you begin to progress in hearing the Lord direct your steps. "Buy the truth, and sell it not; also wisdom, and instruction, and understanding" (Proverbs 23:23). Please read that last portion of again: "also wisdom, and instruction, and understanding." What part of the sitting on the shelf did you not understand? Wisdom from above, from the Lord, is pure and sweet and gentle. Instructions from God are never misunderstood. And understanding means the difference between success and destruction.

But the tide is turning for your ministry. Right? Impatience is the work of a spirit that is bent on your destruction. Go slowly. Some readers will hold on to the familiar and keep what they've got. That's safe and sound judgment, but it does limit you somewhat. Some will sell out or step out of the familiar surroundings and risk going where they've never gone before. That can be dangerous, especially if God hasn't spoken with power and might. And some will be wrapped in wet burlap and carefully placed on a shelf in a dark place to await the Master's call. This is where wisdom, instruction, and understanding begin to shape the lump of clay under that wet burlap. To win the lost is to win yourself.

Shelf time doesn't mean to be unproductive in God's kingdom. Seeking the perfect will of God, you must be willing to explore each and every open door of opportunity that the Lord places before you. Go forward. These words come from the lips of the Lord. We are not to remain still for long. There must first be the call, before there is a going. Even when the fires of disappointment sweep through your heart, you will be challenged in so many ways that you cannot take the loss all at once, but you must press onward to survive. If you are at the point of collapse and you can only see the world from where you stand, go forward. And to most of us in our new world of being former pastors or unscheduled evangelists, it looks and feels like a moonscape without directional signs. With no road maps to guide and no friendly voices to assure you, you think, *What now?* You are in uncharted waters now, but there are others who have made this journey long before you, and by showing you it is possible to turn a stumble into a step, sitting on the shelf can be to your advantage.

CHAPTER 2

Somewhere between AD 64 and AD 67, the Roman emperor Nero began what we have come to know as the first imperial persecution. During this persecution, the apostles Peter and Paul were martyred for their profession of faith of the death, burial, and resurrection of Jesus Christ.

Emperor Domitian of the Romans led a second persecution around AD 95. During this time, approximately 40,000 Christians met their deaths or were tortured. Apostle John was exiled to the island of Patmos during this persecution of the church, and it was here that some historians called apostle John the Revelator because of his writings.

John's resort was actually called Patmos, a small island in the Aegean Sea about 150 miles east of Athens, Greece. It was only ten miles long and six miles wide. A treeless and rocky island inhabited by wild goats and nothing else. What might possibly have been a totally bad experience for John the Revelator became a wonderful experience for those who came afterward and read the Revelation that John recorded.

On one morning when he was praying and was in the spirit on the Lord's Day, the reason for his exile to loneliness and wondering was revealed. Hearing a great voice behind him, John turned to see "one like unto the Son of man" whose eyes were "as a flame of fire" and whose voice was "as the sound of many waters." His countenance, John said, was "as the sun shineth in his strength." And in reaction to this new and unexpected revelation of Jesus, John fell at the feet of the risen Christ Jesus as a dead man. These descriptions can be found in Revelations 1 of the King James Version of the Bible. It sounds strange, but this description of Jesus Christ shows depictions of the power and strength of the Lord Jesus Christ after His resurrection, as John the Beloved recounts his vision. It is an amazing journey that the book of Revelation takes the reader on. But the writer himself was on the shelf at the time, and he was waiting on an open door of opportunity.

This was John's "on the shelf" experience, if you will allow me to call it that. I think it was much more than that. He most likely maintained a close relationship with the Lord throughout the three and a half years of the ministry of Jesus. For John and the other disciples of Christ, it was an adventure that I would call a "school of preparation for things to come." It would seem that after the resurrection of Jesus, and the subsequent outpouring of the power of the Holy Ghost in the upper-room prayer meeting on the day of Pentecost, John the Beloved Disciple continued to have a close relationship with Jesus throughout his consistent and faithful prayer life. In a place where John could have no visitors, he received the greatest visitor that anyone could ever have. Jesus appeared and related some amazing things concerning the coming ages.

Does the Lord realize the beauty in the contrast He finds in our situations? Does He send assistance when we are the weakest, teaching us to trust and to wait upon Him? Has He often supplied our needs when we were the most desperate and when we were at our lowest, lifting us up and giving us hope when there was no hope in sight? On the isle of Patmos, it seems Jesus gave John a glimpse into a glorious future that was on its way. To me, it seemed that Jesus spared no expense to show John the glory and the terror that was approaching the world. No other way was John going to get all of this in the middle of the hustle and bustle of pastoring the churches that sprang up from the day of Pentecost outpouring. A time of loneliness was required. Don't fight it. Embrace it. You may be in for a glorious revelation. Sit tight, and ride out your storm.

When a minister is experiencing a time of need, it is often one of his greatest opportunities for learning more about himself. In the winter of his ministry, when he withdraws from the crowd to meditate and wait upon the Lord to give wisdom, knowledge, and understanding, loneliness is an advantage and not a discouragement. During this time, a person's spirit is humbled by his need, and a humbled heart is much more teachable than a haughty and proud one. The Lord often sends us to the deserted islands for rest or recuperation and sometimes for education. Even though you don't like it, eventually the solitude will reveal God's intense desire to visit with you as friend with friend. Really, we think the Lord is being mean to us, but I assure you He restored me when He put me on the shelf. He is getting you to a place of solitude and separateness that will be the prescription that was written for your particular need. And will you also need the shelving experience after being cut out of the herd and exiled until the Lord chooses to restore you to an active, vibrant, existence? We shall see.

The arm of flesh will fail you, but God never will, not even on the deserted islands of our isolation designed by God's mighty plan. Sometimes you may wonder why God will allow you to experience uncomfortable situations, but it seems that we come to know Him better during these times of peaceful loneliness than during the easy time of living on easy street. During the shelf periods of our ministry, we are more sensitive to His voice than at any other time. When everything is going right, we seem to be self-sufficient. Just let it get hot, and we yelp. God always has a plan for every contingency, from the first time you said yes to His calling. Yielding to the calling that thousands before you have accepted from the Master, to be a fellow laborer with them and to work in the field of souls that they worked in, meant God had a plan for each one of them, as He has a special plan for your life.

He wants to reveal Himself more fully to His servants so He often sends them to the desert places in order to commune with them without interruption. Gulls visited John, but no brethren came to encourage him. Slick rocks, and stinking goats, but in this atmosphere, John heard the Lord speaking to him. At one time in his ministry on the mainland, he was in the big middle of things. Once he was present when miracles were performed and the blind eyes were opened, the deaf ears were unstopped, and the lame walked. Once John was present at the council meetings in Jerusalem, and now he was just an outcast. Rejected by the familiar and forgotten by the faithful, now John the Beloved has been put on the shelf. He has been placed on the back burner of importance, it would appear. But God had a plan for his life. On the shelf can be terribly disconcerting to ego.

Listen. God really has designed a special plan for you. For now, be still, and know that God is God.

There came a time in my life when I felt lonely and thought I had been deserted by all I knew. I was definitely on the shelf of inactivity. I was someone who enjoyed being in the middle of everything that was happening in my church and organization and found myself removed and isolated from the center of activity. I had heard it said, "You can take the preacher out of the church, but you can't take the church out of the preacher." Well, there may be some truth in that statement, but for me, confusion and despair became my companions. I heard these despairing words in my mind more than once: "If you really are the preacher God called you to be, you wouldn't be in this predicament." Satan is called the father of untruth statements. He is the father of such self-degradation. The enemy tried to destroy my plans and came against my thoughts not one day but many more days than I care to remember. But we have an advocate in Jesus Christ. He will suffice. The Word that was with God and was God was in me. I had communication with that Word, and I was not alone.

Now I know that some poor, misguided souls actually do remove themselves from the presence of God. They shelve themselves. Devils and evil men couldn't separate John from the love of God simply by marooning him on an island, and we know that just isn't the case in every situation. If you have shot yourself in the foot, then you'll just have to heal up. But if the will of God is directing your steps, you can rest while knowing that God is guiding you through this downtime in your ministry and on to the place He wants to use your abilities and skills. Now if for some strange reason you have put yourself on a back burner of disgrace, repent, get up, dust yourself off, and march right back up to the front line of action. Go forward again.

The church's own elder turned his loneliness into revelation on the Lord's Day. When his best friend, Jesus, showed him the holy city Jerusalem coming down from heaven adorned like a bride, he even forgot about his pitiful shelter on Patmos. The tempter lost his ability to oppress and depress that old preacher. He was encouraged on the Lord's Day. He probably worshipped the Lord for the great revelation of the victory. You will too.

Exiled and being on the shelf are about the same. And being exiled is not a place to be envied. No one likes to be removed or marooned from his or her family, friends, and associates. No one wants to be put on the shelf, yet such a removal from the mainstream of activity can produce a more productive life than expected. Oh, doesn't that sound lame? When alone and removed from the mainstream of ministry highlights, a person often finds time for self-examination. Right? It's mostly sadness, depression, and the feeling of failure. Not a very desirous place of honor for sure. Once the time of moping around is over, all contacts for possible church services are called, and the résumés have been sent out to the prospective pulpit committees at available churches, the waiting begins. At this point, the mind begins to wander into the land of what-ifs.

What if failure, sickness, adversity, pain, trouble, and sorrow are headed this way? You know experience is a harsh teacher, and very thorough. Every problem we encounter creates a classroom setting through which we may learn. If we will allow it, experiences we encounter during this valley of loneliness of what I've called "sitting on the shelf," waiting on God to open the door of opportunity for us, can teach valuable lessons. When we feel the inactivity after being in the battle of front line ministry, it can seem to be the hardest work you will ever do: the work of being patient. I often must pray for the forgiveness of impatience while waiting on a new door to open up in my experience.

Sometimes you have difficulty sleeping. You may have changes in appetite and blood pressure and experience tense muscles and a weakened immune system. After resigning a church or wondering how long God is going to keep you on the backside of the desert of waiting, you may attempt to return to secular work or even return to higher education, but you'll still have that nagging feeling of being rejected in the back of your mind. After waiting, you will feel less able to concentrate and find yourself distracted by memories and emotions that will flood and disrupt your thinking when you really need to be busy. You will have thoughts of what you could be doing in the church—a church, any church, somewhere—but now all you can do is wait. Leave the consequences up to God. He will work it out. He has a plan. Trust in God's perfect timing. I often remarked that the will of God will drag you down the road to the right place, but as I grow older, I believe that a sensitive heart is conducive to satisfaction in this department. A willing and obedient vessel is what the Lord is producing.

This can lead to discouragement, and it certainly will drain you of ambition and drive when you are no longer the pastor, the favored evangelist, or the bright and shining church worker. Don't be shocked, friend, when you are stunned by the ineptness, the thoughtlessness, and the lack of compassion of some people you thought were allies. Their callousness can be a thorn in your side at times. On the other hand, to be thrilled and deeply touched by the kindness and sensitivity of others is a gift that will be greatly appreciated. Sometimes those you expect to support you the most can't help you at the moment or will not help to meet your needs, while others you weren't that close to before you were put on the shelf will reach out unexpectedly to bless and encourage you. Help may come from the most unexpected sources in times like this. "Don't look a gift horse in the mouth," my father often said. Encouragement is just around the next corner. When God answers your prayer, don't despise the vehicle that God chooses. I remember while walking through this valley that I would go to work each morning with a heart full of hope, hoping a church would call. Maybe the presbyter would call, or just a friend would call, but each morning, there was nothing. It was like the apostle Paul describing the storm that gripped his ship. "And when neither sun nor stars in many days appeared, and no small tempest lay on us, all hope that we should be saved was then taken away" (Acts 27:20).

At my morning break, I would take my coffee and walk out into the gardens to pray or sit beside a small water fountain that cascaded and splashed and made a wonderful backdrop for my melancholy attitude. I prayed and meditated before the Lord anyway. "Oh God, hear me. Just let me see a little sign of recognition that I am being heard." But there never was. Silence wrapped its arms around my soul. Only in my heart did I sense that I did not need to fret because the Lord was not through building something into me for the next level of service in His kingdom, and I would have to be still for a while more.

I chaffed at these times, not knowing that God was working in me a far greater thing than could be found in the activity and busyness of pastoring and preaching. I know now that I was being prepared for a work that only I could do. Was it pride? No. I think that God has certain instruments to perform certain tasks. It is highly possible that you will be placed in a position or called upon to do a work that today you can't imagine yourself occupying, but God can. You may not be ready to do today what God means for you to do tomorrow.

I met a preacher once who had recently stepped back from a very successful ministry. His heart was broken. His face reflected the weariness, and his body posture told a story of battle fatigue. His finances were minimal, and his image as an administrator had been tarnished by gossip. He appeared finished. He was burned out. I tried to cheer him up, I tried to encourage him, and I tried to get him to keep hope and faith alive in his heart, but it was a lost cause. He was headed for the shelf. Weary and depressed, he was giving up all hope of being victorious.

I saw that God was taking this brother down the road to the shelf of education, where he would have things put into his character that no amount of pastoring could do. God can do more in three seconds than a week of Sunday sermons can do, if we would only let Him have His way. I now know that at every new level of ministry I have attained, I have met and fought with new devils. God's preparation has prepared me, faith by faith and step by step, and the conclusion seems to be this: without Him, I can do nothing.

At this junction, you must not focus on the defeat but on the God-given mandate of your calling. "Heal the sick, cleanse the lepers, raise the dead, cast out devils: freely ye have received, freely give" (Matthew 10:8). I saw this same minister several years later at a district ministers' meeting. He was a totally different man from when I had last spoken to him. He was now cheerful, positive, and ready for revival. What had happened? I believe that God had taken him down from the shelf, molded him into a vessel of a specific design, and put him in the place where he was most effective, and the rest is praise and worship to the Master Potter. Wait on the Lord. They who wait will renew their strength.

Now just because you find yourself sitting on the shelf on some other pastor's pew, in a church so large you disappear into the crowd, don't think for one moment that God has lost sight of you. He hasn't. When you wake up to realize that God has "shelved" you for a season, you can experience so many emotions. You may feel relieved from the pressures but then feel guilty about feeling relieved. And truthfully, you may be unable to feel much at all. Even though you start out each day trying to have a normal life, there are still this big hole in your heart and weariness in your steps, and the mountain of responsibility beckons with a cruel reminder: "You still have things to do. Get on with it." So you drag yourself forward another day, embrace the darkness, and await the dawn of the next day.

> Thou wilt keep him in perfect peace, whose mind is stayed on thee: because he trusteth in thee. Trust ye in the Lord forever: for in the Lord Jehovah is everlasting strength. (Isaiah 26:3–4)

When on the shelf becomes part of your experience, you might think that everybody and his brother has heard about your moves and changes, but not all have. Trust me. Even after being out of the loop of what's going on, you will get the odd call from those who haven't heard the news of your ministry change. An evangelist gets your name out of the manual, calls to book a service with you, and then says, "Oh, I didn't know about that. What happened?" And there you go, right back into the whirlpool of emotions that threaten to drag you down deeper and deeper each time you tell the story.

Do you get the sense that your world is anxious for you to get on with your life and no one understands that this *is* your life and you *are* getting on with it? Then other times you pretend and you wear the mask that says everything is fine and perform like a trained seal just to keep what's left of your world of crushed dreams from betraying your true feelings. That's not easy. It seems that we all get a sense of self-worth from the fact that we are pastors, evangelists, or in ministry of some sort, and when that is taken away, we no longer have a mirror to reflect who we are and what we want in life. Now you can only furnish the answers by getting to know yourself again, like you never have before. God is interested in the real you, not where you labor. It is His vineyard, from one end to the other. I love what the preacher A. W. Tozer said.

> God wants worshipers before workers; indeed the only acceptable workers are those who have learned the lost art of worship ... The very stones would praise him if the need arose and a thousand legions of angels would leap to do his will.

Don't lose the art of worship. God is seeking worshippers.

When the prophet Elijah ran from the threats of Queen Jezebel, he found refuge under the shady boughs of a juniper tree. The spirit of a Jezebel is a spirit that hates the minister and the authority God has given to him. That Jezebel spirit can find you wherever you minister. The prophet Elijah was exhausted, mentally burned out, and hungry for answers from God. He fell asleep while exhausted and waiting on God. Could this have been his potter's shelf? His waiting period that happened to be under the juniper bush? Where are you today? On a shelf? Under a juniper tree? Sometimes the rest you receive can be the difference between destruction and restoration. Don't give up; God knows when to withhold visible signs of encouragement and when to give us signs of blessing.

Do you realize that God's Word, which includes His promises of remembrance, are more solid and dependable than any evidence of our five senses? When you've trusted God without a sign, you will appreciate it all the more when He does send one. Delays are not refusals. There is a set time and a set purpose and I believe also a time of deliverance. Hang on. It's coming. God's angel visited him that day and said, "Rise and eat, for the journey is too great for thee." Elijah ate that holy food and went forty days to the mountain of God on that strength. Do you think you can do what must be done, just on the ability of your own strength? No, I think not. You'd better pray yourself empty and read yourself full of God's Word, rather than trust the physical dimension to supply all your wants and wishes.

Remember that it is okay to question God, as long as you don't doubt God. God wants to be in relationship with you no matter what you are feeling. You may be drawn to people who have experienced a loss like yours and can understand some of your feelings and questions, but no one will ever totally understand your question of "Why me, God?" Only someone who has been there before you can truly sympathize with you. Only Jesus can satisfy your soul, because He has a blueprint for your life that is different from everyone else's. Yes, He does. You are special. You are His.

Being on the shelf can actually be a recovery period for you and your family. Family? Oh, did I tell you that no one suffers alone? The wife and the children may also experience some of the same feelings of confusion and feeling out of place. You're not the only one suffering. The family also suffers the feelings of rejection and loneliness when the leader of the family has been "shelved." Time alone does not heal everything; it's what we do with the time of being on the shelf that counts. Try to weave those strands of the past into a new and bright future you never would have planned if God had not put you on the shelf. Think about where you were, where you are, and where you hope to be. Then thank God for the past. Is it over? Or is it just beginning? Praise God for the present. You're alive, at least nearly. Give glory for the future. It hasn't been born yet. Get ready for an exciting opportunity that is surely coming your way. When you go forward, those family members will go with you. They're like a string of boxcars attached to a railroad engine: they react to every stop and go you make. Be merciful to your loved ones, for they are looking to you for their leadership. So lead. They will follow.

Whenever you find yourself on the shelf of God's design, getting through those first few days and weeks can be like winding a ball of string. You start with an end and wind and wind, and then the ball slips through your fingers and rolls across the floor. Some of the work is undone, but not all. You pick the ball up and start over again, but you never have to begin at the end of the string. The ball never completely unwinds; you've made some progress. It is a wearisome business. But one day you will complete the class of training you have been enrolled in by the Head Master and the shelf will be a past school of education and preparation for the new place God has designed just for you. You will graduate. You have not been forgotten. Think of this time of inactivity as a training class and a proving ground for the new opportunity that waits you in the bright, new future that is just around the corner of patience.

One day you may think you're ready for doing "exploits" again for the Lord and returning to your calling, but think about this first. Sam Foss, the poet, was walking down a country lane one hot summer afternoon. Near the foot of a hill, under the shade of a tree, he found a bench. As he sat down wearily, he noticed a sign directing him to a spring. Following the directions, he found the spring with a cup where a traveler could refresh himself. Sitting in the shade, beside the spring, was another bench, and on it was a basket of freshly picked fruit. He wondered who was responsible for such thoughtful and gracious gifts. In discovering the answer, he found that an old man lived near the roadside and kept the benches in repair. He also kept the spring cleaned and the basket filled with fruit when it was in season. The old man had once been a weary and thirsty traveler himself. Now he wanted to help others who might pass by in need of refreshments. Such a thoughtful and unselfish person to want to help a weary traveler along his way I am sure had the marks of a man who had served some time on the shelf in the potter's house. Perhaps he had wondered how he would return to the mainstream of society and do greater than he had ever done before. That's what I'm trying to do. I want to share the thought that anyone who kicks against being on God's shelf needs to learn how to rest, stop resisting the Master's hand, and become faithful about the little things. You may not be as ready as you think you are to rejoin the mainstream. Sit some more in the shade and rest. One day you may be able to encourage someone else who wonders which path to choose or which way to go. Recuperate and enjoy the solitude and beauty of the deserted places. It is here that God reshapes and remakes you from glory to glory in His image, trusting that you will be more like Him, and then sending you out again to make a difference in someone else's life. That is so important.

The scripture reveals,

> My grace is sufficient for thee: for my strength is made perfect in weakness. Most gladly therefore will I rather glory in my infirmities, that the power of Christ may rest upon me. Therefore I take pleasure in infirmities, in reproaches, in necessities, in persecutions, in distresses for Christ's sake: for when I am weak, then am I strong. (2 Corinthians 12:9–10)

And being in the position of waiting for God to use us again, it may be possible that during these dry places in our ministry that we learn more when we lose than when we win.

When the apostle John was on the isle of Patmos, he had time to think. If he'd been at the church in Ephesus or at headquarters in Jerusalem, he might have been so preoccupied with his work that he would not have received the great revelation of the times and things to come. But on that lonely island, there were no activities to detract him from spending that quality time alone with the Lord. He was "in the Spirit," and you may be there, but if you are obedient, submitted, and committed, you will certainly come forth in victory after being on the back burner of activity with the King of Kings. Assuredly, people who come into the presence of the Son of God will not leave the same way they came; they will leave as changed individuals. Many times I wished for the simpler moments in the life of my ministry, quiet times alone with my coffee and newspaper and with my family in good health and nothing to worry about. No wants, with plenty of everything. Yet there was always that nagging feeling at the back of my conscience telling me to "draw near, draw near." It was probably a warning to get prepared for the day I might be on a shelf somewhere. I'm sure it is what it I believe it to be today, calling me to prepare for the days ahead that would test me severely. God may even call you aside where "He maketh you to lie down in green pastures: where He leadeth you beside the still waters" (Psalm 23:2). Yes, Lord, obedience is required, and submission is the answer.

God always wants to give us better than we want for ourselves. He looks ahead and around the corner and sees the need before you even know what the problem will be. The writing of the apostle Paul to the Ephesian church said, "Now unto him that is able to do exceeding abundantly above all that we ask or think, according to the power that worketh in us" (Ephesians 3:20). When my ministry went on the shelf, I found plenty of time to be in the Spirit and to draw near. Especially with all those pesky bills coming due seemingly on the same day. And believe me: at the end of the month, there was always more month left than money. When these moments of pressure and stress would build, I needed to retreat to the islands of separateness. Here is where

I really got with the program. God would meet with me there in those desperately lonely hours. He never forsook me. He won't abandon you either. I wondered sometimes if He would meet me, but He always did. He is probably already waiting for you at the place of your prayer. Go to Him. If living by faith is unsettling to you, you'd better reexamine your calling. It is a walk of faith, by faith.

We can then begin to see Him as He really is. Instead of goat paths, we can see the future with golden streets. Instead of locked in by a sea of troubles, we are surrounded by that sea of peace in the Holy Spirit. Preacher, don't fret. Sons and daughters of the Spirit, don't worry. Quit wiggling around on the altar of sacrifice. Stay on the altar. Stay in the fire. Present yourself totally, and completely, into the hands of the Master to do with as He sees fit. "I beseech you therefore, brethren, by the mercies of God, that ye present your bodies a living sacrifice, holy, acceptable unto God, which is your reasonable service" (Romans 12:1).

The Old Testament priests used the horns on the corners of the altar to tie the sacrifice to the altar so that it would be properly positioned and would be completely consumed in the fire. Stay in the fire. God wants all of you. Being on the shelf is a lot like being consumed on the altar of sacrifice. Sit tight. Something is happening in you, through you, and for you. The victory will become apparent very soon. We could always feel sorry for ourselves and simply fade away from the presence of the Lord, but that is not God's grand design for a preacher on the shelf. God cannot use the pity-party preacher. Pity isn't faith any more than sandpaper is smooth. Crying over "poor me" isn't going to convince the Lord to change His agenda for you. Allow the transformation to be completed. Trust Him, obey, believe, and say, "I believe, God." He will wait until your attitude changes from self-pity to worship and praise, despite the circumstances. Then God moves. Remember He loved you before you loved Him.

God hears the prayer of faith and the prayer of praise. I believe that the Lord is drawn by our needs, but He is moved by our faith. And when the minister cannot pray a prayer of faith, he must pray that prayer of praise. Jeremiah tells us,

> If thou hast run with the footmen, and they have wearied thee, then how canst thou contend with horses? And if in the land of peace, wherein thou trustest, they wearied thee, then how wilt thou do in the swelling of Jordan. (Jeremiah 12:5)

Or in plain, everyday language, he says if you can't take the heat, how come you're still in the kitchen?

Have you got what it takes to go to the next level of your ministry? It may take grit in your craw and you will need a spirit of determination, or you will give up and throw in the towel when the discourager whispers in your ear, "You can't take this anymore."

I woke up one day to discover I wasn't in the mainstream of things. I wasn't a mover or a shaker any longer, not that I moved more than anybody else—and most of my shaking was probably caffeine. Dump trucks can be movers, and saltshakers can be poured out, so what was my problem? I was tired of being on the sidelines and watching everyone else get with the program. I wanted to get on with my calling. I was tired of just sitting on the shelf in God's pottery room. A wise saying is "If you can't run with the big dogs, stay on the porch." This potter's shelf might just be where you are supposed to be right now. The steps of a good man and a good woman are still ordered by the Lord, aren't they? And so are the stops. So here you are right on target. John the Revelator could have really been down in the dumps. He could have thought himself forsaken by God's will, passed by and passed over, while someone else seemed to be the anointed one and someone else was being blessed and chosen, but he didn't. He penned the words to one of the most intriguing books in our Bible while he was on the shelf. Marooned on an island, rejected by the political scenery, and hated by the religious leadership, he was in the Spirit. God was using Him.

The preacher who finds himself on the shelf at a most critical point in his ministry must remember that Jesus was a man of sorrows. While feeling that we are only at our best in a performance when we feel our best physically, it is to forget that we walk by faith and not by sight. Can you hear a still, soft voice whispering lowly and softly in your heart to stay the course when you want to quit? The opposite can be true sometimes. We just have to decide. We must choose. It will happen. Our nights will turn to day, our storms will turn to sunshine, and we will one day come off the shelf and onto the potter's wheel. Then there will be "Lights, camera, and action!"

Lift up your head. Your redemption is drawing near. The island of Patmos was a prison for John, but it became a place of freedom when he got ahold of the Revelation. We must choose to maintain a spiritual balance instead of a roller coaster of frustration. Worshipping God rather than the problems we encounter while existing on this shelf of spiritual growth can create the atmosphere of answered prayer, and that is by a choice. Focus on the answer for a while instead of the problem. Remember the secrets of success will not work unless you do. Maintain your consistent prayer, and keep the Word fresh in your heart. A sweet spirit and a peaceful attitude will go a long way when everything is upside down and swirling around you like a flood. No matter what, smile—if it kills you.

CHAPTER 3

The Egyptians, who were famous for their beautifully glazed earthenware, are credited with having invented the potter's wheel. Among the Hebrews, pottery was a known art, and once they were settled in Canaan, they developed distinctive forms of pottery. Before the potter's wheel came into common use, all vessels were shaped by hand. By the prophet Jeremiah's time, the wheel was in general use. Dry clay, dug out of the field, was steeped in water and further softened by the potter's feet as he stepped up and down in the clay. After being shaped, vessels were dried and then baked in a furnace.

The word *ceramic* comes from the Greek word for "potter." The following passage of scripture plainly describes a potter's craft as seen through the eyes of the prophet Jeremiah.

> The word which came to Jeremiah from the Lord, saying, Arise, and go down to the potter's house, and there I will cause thee to hear my words. Then I went down to the potter's house, and, behold he wrought a work on the wheels. And the vessel that he made of clay was marred in the hand of the potter: so he made it again another vessel, as seemed good to the potter to make it. Then the word of the Lord came to me, saying, O house of Israel, cannot I do with you as this potter? saith the Lord. Behold, as the clay is

in the potter's hand, so are ye in mine hand, O house
of Israel. (Jeremiah 18:1–6)

The power of the Holy Spirit is the only power that can transform a
human being completely and perfectly. No social worker can provide
enough psychological input to transform a person from the inside out
the way the Holy Spirit does. The potter's wheel is the instrument
used by the potter to effect the changes in clay that will produce
the desired usefulness of a vessel. Similarly, without the presence of
the Holy Spirit, the "fervent prayer of a righteous man," spoken of
in James 5:16, accomplishes nothing. The letter kills, but the Spirit
is what gives the life. You may have the feeling you've been given
orders, but you don't know where to do them. While you're in this
"boot camp" of waiting on the Lord, the holy anointing will guide
you, teach you, and supply all you need during this time of learning.
You may be a real "rock'em, sock'em" prayer warrior, but unless you
get busy again praying in the Spirit, you're going to be a long time on
this shelf of learning.

A man's gift will make room for him and bring him before great men,
but it's hard to pray when all you feel is frustration. And it's hard to
sing when all you feel is depression. But when you remember the
goodness of the Lord and all He's done for you, your soul cries out,
"Hallelujah." Thank God for choosing you to be prepared in such a
special way that requires you to take a side journey away from the
mainstream of kingdom activity. Thank God for the love and grace
that cascades down from above. Your abilities and natural giftings will
bring you to the right place at the right time, and by the way, there is
no such thing as luck. Preparation and opportunity create the spark
of new beginnings at the intersection of surprise. Pray in the Spirit.
You'll gain more ground. Believe me: it took a while to quit having my
pout soup at my own personal pity-party. You can't suck your thumb
and worship God at the same time either. You may take three steps
forward and slide back two, but at least that one step you gained is

closer to the goal. Getting off the shelf and back into the mainstream of usefulness in the ministry does not have any shortcuts. You will go the complete course if you are to succeed.

Although regarded as an inferior craft among Egyptian artisans, the potter still provided articles that were useful for many applications in the life of their community. In bondage, Israel was forced to accomplish this task as brickmaking slaves. Potters usually lived near the source of their clay. You can imagine how each potter was proud of his productions, for every potter praised his own pot and the potter is envious of the potter, the smith of the smith. The potter's field, purchased with the money Judas received for betraying his Master, was likely a field that had been worked out by a potter. It probably was good for nothing but a burial place where strangers, such as Romans and proselytes, were buried after all the useful clay had been removed. The potter's products touched the lives of every person before the days of modern conveniences. Long before Tupperware, fine china plates, and crystal goblets, there was pottery. Some of the objects were elaborate in design, and some were just useful and simple yet functional for everyday usage.

Some very expressive biblical metaphors are taken from the craft of the potter, as a survey of the twenty-two times it is mentioned proves. First of all, the potter's skill, as he molded the clay to his purpose or need, typified the sovereignty of God in shaping the characters and destinies of both nations and individuals—sometimes without their knowledge. The ability of the potter to mold the clay in his hands to any pattern or purpose he might please is used by many writers to symbolize God's mind in dealing with the people He called His own. It is God's right to deal with saints and sinners alike, according to His own perfect counsel. "But now, O LORD, thou art our father; we are the clay, and thou our potter; and we all are the work of thy hand" (Isaiah 64:8). Then there are several allusions to the fragile nature of clay, symbolizing as it does man's brittle qualities. A vessel, no matter how beautifully formed, is quickly broken once it has been fired. God, as the divine Potter, formed Adam from the dust. He is able to smite the wicked, as one who would smash a piece of pottery, but God is merciful. Today His grace doesn't give us what we deserve because God isn't into the destruction of men and women but in the restoration and deliverance business of their eternal well-being. I'm so glad He cares for us enough to pick up the broken pieces of our lives and give us that second chance that no one else cared to give us. Oh, how He loves you and me.

In Estes Park, Colorado, there was once a giant tree. Naturalists say that this tree was over five hundred years old when it died. When Christopher Columbus landed at San Salvador, it was already a full-grown tree. Five hundred winters had piled their snows about its roots; five hundred summers had directed their heat and storms upon it. Eleven times it had been struck by lightning, and each time it healed over the scar. Three times there were landslides, but each time, the old tree had dug its roots in a little deeper and held its place. For five hundred years, the old tree defied nature and laughed at the storms, the winds, the lightning strikes, the cold, and the heat, but something took it down. Naturalists say it was a tiny beetle that a child could have crushed between its thumb and finger. It had slipped under the bark one day and quietly began to work.

This tiny beetle did what the tremendous forces of nature could not accomplish. This is so typical of our lives in the ministry. It's not the great forces or the great opportunities that threaten us. It's always the loss of our vision and the loss of our focus upon the work that God has set before us. When prayer has ceased to be an obsession and becomes a bother, and when the daily grind of life becomes monotonous, then the moments of inactivity and those fearful interludes of slack times come. This is when it seems that God places your world on a shelf in a darkened, damp, backroom somewhere, but this is not the end. You begin again to refocus and regain the vision that God had originally designed for your life. Just as the tiny beetle destroyed that great tree, it was probably just a little distraction that mowed you down to your knees. On the shelf actually may reset the default switch that could restart your original purpose God had designed for your ministry and your desire to serve the Lord, as it was in the beginning. The work that God started in you is going to be finished, if you will allow it to be finished.

Preacher, Christian worker, evangelist, you are in the hands of the most skilled Potter this world has ever known. Apostle Paul told Timothy to make "full proof of your ministry" (2 Timothy 4:5). That was on my mind when I talked with a very wise and experienced minister several years ago about being on the shelf during the testing times of my ministry. He told me,

> A man's gift will make room for him. You see so many men trying to make room for their supposed gifting long before they will submit fully to follow the sensitive leading of the Holy Spirit. Making "full proof" of your ministry is easier said than done. Let God develop the opportunities. You must focus on the prayer and fasting.

I have found that ministers are a funny breed of creature. They get these great ideas about how it's going to be and then set out to make it so. Then God comes along and tears it all down because they were hoping to bend God's will to their desires rather that fulfilling the will of the Lord. It's this way sometimes; we try to meet the need without realizing the personalities behind those needs. A man's character must be settled and mature. Long before he wins the world, he must first win himself. Then and there, God gets the firstfruits, for a man's true character is what he is when no one is observing him. Character is described in one dictionary as "public reputation, and qualities that distinguishes one person from another." First Chronicles 4:9

said that Jabez was more honorable than his brothers. Something set him apart from the rest of his family. I think it could have been his character or his personality. It certainly set him apart for things that were beyond the normal realm of things called "spiritual." I've heard that hardness makes character. At least it seemed so from my perspective. Hard times and faithfulness can create a very determined personality. It can.

In all these troubles, has your character changed? Has your personality remained constant? Remember when you were little in your own eyes? Once a dear sister in Christ told me, "Brother Jimmy, stay humble, and God will use you." She couldn't have been a truer prophet.

Humbling yourself in the sight of God is the best way to be exalted by God. This scripture puts it into perspective for us.

> Likewise, ye younger, submit yourselves unto the elder. Yea, all of you be subject one to another, and be clothed with humility: for God resisteth the proud, and giveth grace to the humble. Humble yourselves therefore under the mighty hand of God, that he may exalt you in due time. (1 Peter 5:5–6)

God pleads, "If my people which are called by my name, will humble themselves and pray ... turn from their wicked ways ..." (2 Chronicles 7:14). Take the word "turn" for example. *Turn* in the Hebrew has been explained to mean "to go back to the point of origin" in the English. The shelf experience sometimes is merely the turning and refocusing of a man's point of destination. It can be simply a reviving of his vision from the point of his beginnings. Or it can be similar to going back to the altar, repenting, and starting all over again—reinventing the wheel, if you will. Integrity of character is when the character of an individual is not divided and is whole. No split personality here. Rev. T. F. Tenney said in his book *Some Things I Wish I'd Known* that "without integrity, you may reach the heights but not true success, impress the crowd for a while but not the Master, soar like a skyrocket but finally descend like a burned out stick." What good is success in the ministry without the approval of the King of Kings? God is definitely committed to the character of a man and not to his charisma. Charisma is the ability to win the devotion of others, while character is that moral strength that you won't compromise for anything or anybody.

The mountaintop is a great place for seeing long distances, but the valley we descend into immediately after the vision of great places and great things is the only way for traveling. Loneliness is sometimes the only companion on such journeys. Without the purpose of direction and the perfect will of God to build upon, a preacher is only shouting into the wind. We do the what without knowing the why. I'm sweeping around my own doorstep now. We ask,

> But God, why does the shelving experience have to come at this time? Let it be somebody else who really needs shelving. God, let's talk about this "making full proof of your ministry" thing.

"But watch thou in all things, endure afflictions, do the work of an evangelist, make full proof of thy ministry" (2 Timothy 4:5). Imagine the boldness of some folks as they resist the act of being put on the shelf. I might hope to persuade you to not follow this line of thinking.

> Dear Lord, couldn't I just make a little down payment now and have the balance due paid out over several years? Sort of like an installment plan? No? Okay. Lord, You know best. On the shelf will be my place until you are satisfied."

Find your place at the foot of Calvary and commit your dreams and desires one more time. "How can I possibly learn anything sitting here on this shelf?" I asked myself. "While here I sit in this pew, holding a songbook instead of being up on the platform leading a service, I feel like I have been caught between two places and the breath is being squeezed out of my body. Besides, I could do as good a job as that guy's doing."

I carried on a running dialogue with the Lord that morning in church.

> What's that, Lord? You think I could do with a dose of my own medicine? Now that's not fair! Am I learning anything? Sure, but I don't feel fulfilled at all just singing, worshiping, giving in the offering, clapping my hands, and watching hairdos and babies cry. And, oh Lord, how long? Weeping may endure for the night, but will it be all night, Lord?

My moaning and groaning prayer got me nowhere. Please let me reassure you there are no shortcuts to victory lane. None whatsoever.

What's that I hear? The strange news that reports that the wounded preacher is now sitting on the shelf of inactivity, hidden from all activity. The once great leader who had already qualified before by position of leadership in a pastorate, or ministry of helps, is now being proven on the world's most grueling testing ground of life: the potter's shelf. I heard an old proverb that said, "When you need a helping hand, look at the end of your arm." Sometimes we try to go it alone, when we are in the position of being between pastorates or ministries, and find that we are lacking so much, especially in the realm of a friend. You need somebody safe and trustworthy to talk to and express frustrations and concerns to without fear that it will be broadcast all over kingdom come.

Just where are all those helping hands when you really need them? Scriptures tell us to "seek His face," and if we are seeking His hands all the time, we might miss the part about sitting down at His feet and choosing the better thing. Come on. Choose to sit at His feet, seek His face, and let Him have His way in your life. I heard that He chooses our rests for us. I hated taking naps as a child, but after Mother convinced me to lie still for a few minutes, I awakened refreshed and full of get-up-and-go. It was just what I needed. Mother knew best.

Our Savior loves us much more than a mother. He wants the best for us, and time on the shelf can be the best refreshment ever. He knows just what we need—right when we need it the most. Quit kicking against His suggestions. He makes you to lie down in green pastures, even if you don't want to. After Moses dropped the ball in the beginning of his ministry to the Israelites, killing an Egyptian didn't enhance his reputation very much. But God didn't give up on this future leader. He just sent Him to a desert place to learn some powerful things about this God of Israel. He invited Moses to kick off his shoes, stay a while, and learn something in the desert place of loneliness that he could have never learned anywhere else in the world.

Just as you are learning now, God is trying to talk to you. Listen. Look. Learn. The burning bush is waiting on you. Why not kick off your shoes too? You may be standing on holy ground.

Jesus told the man whose child was possessed by evil spirits to just believe. One particular story I read about this miracle says that the desperate father answered the question Jesus had asked him by saying, "Lord, I believe. Help me when my faith falls short." When we feel like giving up, could it be because our faith is falling just short of where it needs to be? Not because we don't have faith but because we've tried and tried and fatigue leads to frustration, which leads to discouragement. And that had better lead you to an altar or you will become another casualty of burnout. You may just become another statistic for your organization's quarterly paper to report to all of the self-sufficient minutemen who armchair quarterback yet another explanation of failure from where they are ministering and adopt the "He just didn't have what it took" attitude. Let Jesus be the bridge over the canyon of impossibility. If your faith is falling short, I suggest allowing the mercy of Jesus to bridge the gap of what is going on in your life and bring your faith and your heart where it needs to be under the protection of His love. Decide now to trust what God's Word says about you and not what the enemy is whispering in your ear. God is trying to show you that you are valuable to Him and the He cares very much about you and your ministry. He will bring you out again and show you His favor and blessings until you will not be able to believe it at all.

There are several studies about ministers and the growing crisis of dropping out of the calling of the ministry work and returning to secular vocations nowadays. I've read some stories that were so sad. Let it suffice to say that the majority of them agreed nearly 100 percent that a very large percentage of seminary graduates entering the ministry leave within five years and an even larger percent of all pastors will not stay to retirement. This study also found that some clergy who left the ministry ran as high as 90 percent for those having served twenty years or more. These ministers apparently left to preserve what was left of their families, their sanity, their health, and their faith.

You could be suffering from unusually high expectations from a congregation. If so, get down on your knees and pray until you have found the face of God. Quit seeking the conclusion to the issue, and seek His face. If His people will seek His face, He will hear them. Stop checking His hands for your answers. It's in the face and not the hands. You may be on the shelf, but you can also talk with the Lord; still He answers those who call on Him. Crawl up in His lap of mercy and stay in those arms of love until you are able to go forward again.

Remember you are His first love, not a pulpit committee's pick of the litter.

If only there were those who would reach out and touch the lives of our needy ministers who are waiting on God to open doors to new opportunities. These encouragers would be sensitive and gentle; they would be filled with patience and compassion. If only they could counsel our counselors. Ministers need encouragers. The apostle Paul had his Barnabas, but whom do you have?

We often lack the imagination and drive needed to give just that little bit of extra help that could go such a long way toward healing and encouraging someone who has resigned from a church position or failed in some way that displeased a congregation. We might bother, get in the way, or hinder in some way. Nonsense. Whatever the need might be, to encourage someone is very real and needed. It is also to be like Jesus. You can salvage someone's ministry by just a kind word or a friendly pat on the back. Reach out and touch someone as they pass your way. You'll find you're not that busy to hear their heart cry. Perhaps they are wearing the plastic mask that says, "Everything is wonderful," while all the time their life is falling to pieces. They may be passing by you this moment and your words can heal and calm, so reach out, brother or sister encourager, and touch the lonely and the hurting as they pass by. You can make a difference, if you will let God use you.

I was once so discouraged and filled with thoughts of quitting. I was once ready to forget the calling God had placed on my life and just return to the place where I first began. I remember the hand of a sweet pastor's wife as she placed her hand on my shoulder one cold Sunday morning and said, "Lord, touch this young man of God and give him the strength to do Your work." It worked. I returned to my calling to do all that I could through God's power to the pulling down of strongholds, and I'm still working for the Lord. Thank God for encouragers, for they come in all shapes and sizes and ages. God uses willing people to reach out and touch the wounded and sensitive places of our lives. God uses willing vessels. You can be one, if you are willing.

My desire for you is that you will receive strength and insight into where you are and where you could be heading to as God opens or closes doors in your life and ministry. I pray that encouragement will flow into you the way it did my heart that Sunday morning so long ago. As I look back down that long road of history in my personal life, I can see the need for words of wisdom, acts of kindness, and strength from friendships that won't quit when the going gets rough. I want to reach out to people reading this book and know that perhaps they will one day help someone else as they move toward that anointed destiny they were designed to fulfill. It will be done as long as you submit yourself to the lonely place you may be living in today.

CHAPTER 4

"Faith Never Struggles; It Rests." This was the title of a sermon I preached one Sunday morning in 1990. I've used that theme many places where I was invited to minister. Faith is never struggling with the problem. It rests with the solution always. Sometimes it seems that in order for us to wrestle with a dilemma, we must get into a fix or a struggle to bring about the solution. Now you know that's not faith. That's not even close to faith.

Faith is the substance of things hoped for, not the substance of things struggled with. Not something that someone says you can or cannot have. Faith is the substance. *Substance.* Not wishful thinking but substance. Faith is not maybe so; faith *is*. The actual, tangible reality of a situation is its substance. All things in the world we live in have substance. The laws of physics and dynamics bind this world that we live in with what we call the five senses. Sight, smell, hearing, touch, and taste are the five senses we lean so heavily upon to inform us of what is going on in our little corner of the world. We know about substance. But what do we know about faith substance? The very thing that occupies the space where you are right now is faith substance. This is unseen, so understand that when I say "substance" I'm referring to literal and physical reality by faith. "Now faith is the substance of things hoped for, the evidence of things not seen" (Hebrews 11:1). When you do exercise your faith, it will demand an answer. Go get ready to celebrate a victory. It is coming. Jesus told His followers that if you believed what you were saying by faith, you would have it. If you believe that, you can begin the celebration right now.

Is it possible to have faith and actually put something to work you can't feel, see, or touch? How can something have substance and not occupy space? Now we are getting to the point. Even if you don't feel anything, feeling doesn't change the fact that faith isn't working. We walk by faith, not by sight or feelings. Paul didn't state in Hebrews 11:1 just whose faith was the substance, did he? He just said faith is the substance ... I would say that the faith that is the substance of things hoped for must come from a source outside our limited ability. I'm saying that it takes the faith of God to actually speak something into existence from a state of nothingness. We each have been given a measure of that God-creating faith. And it'll take the Holy Spirit to create the substance that will in turn bring to pass the things we are hoping and believing for. You have been given the authority to speak by faith what is not, as though it does now exist. Man's faith is hopeful; God's faith is absolute. Put your trust in God's faith, and whatsoever you say—whether it's to a mountain or to a fig tree—has to move or dry up.

Be careful now. Patience is the governor that controls the speed of receiving, and that is a virtue. So don't get out of joint if what you're hoping for doesn't pop up on your radar the moment you brilliantly devise a plan to get yourself back on track and in the loop of spiritual activity. We are professionals at helping God devise just the perfect plan. But God doesn't need our input, and He just goes past us on His way to something bigger and better than we would ever dream up or ask for ourselves. Are you hoping? Waiting? Watching? Struggling? Try resting. Just what do you propose to do today? Drape yourself over the back of a chair like a shirt and say, "Okay, Lord, here I am. Use me today for Your kingdom, if You want, or I can even assist You." No, that's not what the doctor is ordering at all.

> For we are saved by hope: but hope that is seen is not
> hope: for what a man seeth, why doth he yet hope for?
> But if we hope for that we see not, then do we with
> patience wait for it. (Romans 8:24–25)

We are to wait with patience for the thing for which we are hoping. And when we see that which we are waiting to appear, we cease to hope and begin to rejoice. Yes, rejoice. Rejoice, stand still, and see the salvation of the Lord at work. I believe you ought to get out the turkey and dressing pan and have a real Thanksgiving Day just because you know and believe that the answer is on the way.

The language of praise with which to build the foundation of yet another miracle is "Praise Him." So let everything which has breath praise the Lord. Praise the Lord. From his book *It Was on Fire When I Lay Down on It,* Robert Fulghum made a very valid point.

> I believe that imagination is stronger than
> knowledge—That myth is more potent than history.
> I believe that dreams are more powerful than facts—
> That hope always triumphs over experience—That
> laughter is the only cure for grief. And I believe that
> love is stronger than death.

Good for you, Robert, but sometimes this old shelf I've been sitting on gets splintery and I want a change of view. Can I endure until my scenery changes and the old becomes new? Hang on. A change is in the works for you.

I read somewhere that up on the high bluffs of Ulm, Germany, overlooking the Danube River in the foothills of the Bavarian Alps, lived a maker of artificial limbs named Hans Ludwig Babblinger. One day he constructed wings with his skills from the materials in his shop. Finally he tried his invention on the slopes of the Alps, where up currents were plentiful. It worked, and as he jumped from a high hill, he soared safely down to the crowd who witnessed his daring feat. The city leaders wanted to impress King Ludwig in 1594 with this man who had mastered the wind with his invention to fly, so they convinced Babblinger to show the king his ability. Not wanting to put the king to any discomfort, they chose the bluffs of the Danube River for the demonstration because it was closer to the town than the bluffs. But the winds there were all down currents. So Babblinger stood ready, waved to the king, threw himself into the air, and promptly went down like a rock into the river.

With dreams, wings, and heart smashed and broken, rejected and ridiculed, he never regained a stable existence. This was an idea before its time.

God never gives up. Man does. Hans gave up on himself. Today pilots never think of Babblinger and the crash of wings and his self-esteem— or broken dreams and smashed ideas. At 30,000 feet, a 747 jet slants up toward 38,000 feet over Ulm, but if somehow Hans Babblinger could be called from his grave, you could tell him,

"Don't be ashamed, Hans. Man does fly."

The way we see ourselves isn't necessarily the way we are. How does the Lord see you? Self-rejection over what is going on in your ministry is not an indicator of your self-worth to the Lord. It takes time for an oyster to make a pearl. That oyster is blessed with a tiny irritant that is coated with nacre over and over again until a small, perfectly formed sphere is nestled in the folds of the oyster's body. The value comes from the type of irritant that it began with in the first place. God's timing is always perfect. Never premature and never late.

The shelf of testing, training, and teaching reveals so much, if only we are willing to wait and learn its secrets. You probably feel like you are going to produce a kidney stone, but God has a plan and you will be a valuable asset to His kingdom. You may be developing a pearl of great price, and only God knows what the results will be.

There are some men and women who dream of things we never think about. They speak of ways to reach a lost and dying world with new and innovative ideas we have never envisioned. These folks are the dreamers who will try again and again to stretch the impossibility into the possibility. These are the risk takers, the ones who will try to make it work in spite of failed attempts. These visionaries will try until their ideas really do work. They often end up on the shelf waiting for God to open the doors of opportunity. But they are always willing to try one more time. Being on the shelf can have a happy ending. If an arrow is being pulled backward, it is going to be launched forward, so keep your eye on the target. Going forward can be a journey of joy, if you will only look for the blessings along the way. And I assure you there are blessings you cannot envision that your King has thoughtfully prepared for you along the pathway you are traveling. Watch for those surprises He has prepared for you.

CHAPTER 5

Thomas a' Kempis said, "Why, then, are you afraid to take up your cross, which leads to the kingdom? In the cross is salvation; in the cross is life, in the cross is strength of mind; in the cross is joy of spirit." Are you so afraid to pick up that cross and follow Jesus? After all, you do want to enter that kingdom. If the only way into that kingdom is with a cross, then you had better start praying, "Give me my cross." Salvation, life, strength of mind, and joy of spirit all lie within the shadow of the Cross of Calvary. Thank God for the blood. You may be down today, but help is on the way. Dark clouds may cover your sky, but God is going to answer you by and by. Let's pause for a moment and praise Him.

> And I beheld, and I heard the voice of many angels round about the throne and the beasts and the elders: and the number of them was ten thousand times ten thousand, and thousands of thousands; Saying with a loud voice, Worthy is the Lamb that was slain to receive power, and riches, and wisdom, and strength, and honour, and glory, and blessing. (Revelations 5:11–12)

You and I are living for this kingdom, preparing for it, preparing others for it, and looking toward that great homecoming with extreme anticipation. In order to get from the shelf to the potter's wheel, one must go through the process of moving spiritually. Many fall into the trap of exhaustion while trying to do it on their own, allowing their conscience to become the judge of a performance that is the result of trying to obey God in the first place. Here is when the stagnation of spiritual surroundings paralyzes the hope in their heart and speech. The critic who sits in the seat of self-judgment is always ready to criticize or to applaud but never willing to risk the possibility of any real participation to lend a constructive analysis.

The true called-of-God minister cannot merely be an observer of the power of God in his personal ministry only. He must experience the actual participation of the exchange of power between the holding stage of preparation and the engagement of valuable soul-saving intercession. That is when the power of prayer becomes the buffer between the five senses and the faith that God will finish the work that He has begun.

Don't judge yourself harshly. Prayer time is the lifeline of being on the shelf. Don't miss this moment of reconciliation. It makes all the difference. Without prayer, you probably will not go beyond being on the shelf. You must pray diligently, fervently, and faithfully, but you must maintain that prayer life; it is your life now. Waiting on God is not easy sometimes. Prayer gains momentum, and when that occurs, it is easier to keep on praying than when you first began.

Ministers on the stage of life, who are God called and God anointed, are ground down into the fine dust of rejection by well-meant intentions of offers for future positions that somehow evaporate as someone else is chosen. After thirty-eight years at the pool of Bethesda, the lame man was asked by Jesus, "Why?" His reply was "Someone else beats me to the pool." Jesus told him, "Arise." Start moving. Don't just be stirred. Be moved. Are we not taught to lean not to our own understanding? And does the scripture not teach that there is a way that seems right to a man? The footlight critics of your mind will grind you to powder with their grindstone opinions and sharp barbs of advice. And when those critics speak, you must pray again, "Lord, Thy kingdom come, my kingdom go." Stay humble, submitted, and committed to the Word that God gives. Hope is about to be revealed, and you are going to rejoice with great joy.

I believe that the landscape of our ministerial history is strewn with the remains of great preachers who let being on the shelf bring them down to ruin. Like great nations that had momentary lapses in their forward momentum, refusing to refocus their vision, they became victims of their past, destined to repeat history, because they allowed the downtime of being on the shelf to destroy the faith that was designed to prepare them for a "greater than this" ministry. The Romans ruled the entire world with their iron fists of rule, and the Greeks gave the world its first glimpse of democracy. Those civilizations shared with the world men such as Socrates, Plato, and Aristotle. The ancient Mayans performed brain surgery long before our greatest surgeons and excelled in mathematics that caused Einstein to ponder. This included astronomy that is still used today. And they built incredible networks of irrigation canals. What happened to these people?

Historians have grappled with the question in depth, but to my simple mind, it seemed that these ancient superpowers refused to sit still while the plan of God was draped over them to measure them for the future.

Are there no new discoveries to enlighten the lives of mankind? Are there no new inventions to alleviate the pain and suffering from diseases and to show the pathway to healthier lifestyles? Are there no new revelations for peace relations among the peoples of this world? From the dark hills of the land of the potter's shelf comes a clear sound, a fresh illumination, a clearing away of the shadows of misunderstandings, and fears of destruction. God has a fresh and new thing that will refresh and encourage those He is using in this day and time. "Behold, I will do a new thing; now it shall spring forth; shall ye not know it? I will even make a way in the wilderness, and rivers in the desert" (Isaiah 43:19). Those who repent, humble themselves, and allow changes to be made within their souls, from the experience of being on the shelf, will one day emerge as champions of faith to give glory to the Almighty for His love. The shadow of things that could be changed by these present actions of God's intervention will prove undoubtedly to be the amazing answer to your life's riddling questions.

Your character formed by the scars of life that faithfulness now covers like a protective shell will emerge as a tribute to the wisdom of God's plan to submit you to the testing and loneliness period of the shelf of the potter's house. When you're in between appointments for the Lord, you'll have a disappointment here, a sorrow there, maybe a victory today, and a defeat tomorrow, but they'll all go into the mixing pot to make you what God wants you to be. Those scars and defeats and sitting on God's potter's shelves become the marks of a beautiful spirit in a messenger of the Lord. Humble, sweet, meek—that is what I think Jesus must have been like. Never bitter, brassy, or outspoken but ever bearing in your body the marks of the Lord Jesus that will result in the attitude of gratitude that cannot be mistaken by anyone.

You may already know this little story about a tightrope walker named Blondin, but I want to retell it for you. In 1857, Blondin stretched a two-inch steel cable across the gorge of Niagara Falls. He picked up a sack of sand weighing about 180 pounds and carried it across the falls. Then he asked the onlookers, "How many of you believe that I can actually carry a person across the gorge?" Many people in the crowd indicated that they thought he could do it. Then Blondin called out, "Which one of you will climb on my shoulders and let me carry you across the falls?" Suddenly there was silence. Everyone wanted to see him carry a person across the gorge, and many believed he could. But nobody wanted to put his life in Blondin's hands. Sometime later, Blondin did carry a man across Niagara Falls. His manager. "You must not trust your own feelings but mine," Blondin told his manager as they prepared for the crossing. "You will feel like turning when we don't need to turn. And if you trust your feelings, we will both fall. You must become part of me." And this is what trusting the Master's guidance is all about. You must allow Him to lead you through the places of doubt and fear and trust His hand to bring you safely over to the place of production and activity once again. The feeling of helplessness is often experienced whenever you are just waiting on God to open the door of opportunity. It seems like the enemy slips into your thinking whenever there are weariness and fatigue from the stress and strain of ups and downs involved in the exercise of faith. And being faithful can be tiring indeed. Maybe that's why the Bible says for us to not be weary in well doing. You may want to turn or lean this way or that when you don't need to lean or turn. And if we trust our own feelings, we may fall if we don't become one with the Lord's desires and will. Isaiah said it this way: "They that wait upon the Lord shall renew their strength" (Isaiah 40:31). Apostle Paul said, "And let us not be weary in well doing: for in due season we shall reap, if we faint not" (Galatians 6:9).

The refocusing of your attention at times will be the renewing of your strength and not fainting. Sometimes the only reason we keep hanging on is just to keep our heads above the water. How long can you tread water anyway? I find that, personally, my strength is about as enduring as my attention span, and when I try to strengthen my grip on the things of hope, I feel the slipping sensation of defeat. What's going on? I must learn to trust that He has a grip on me. "Rejoice not against me, O mine enemy: when I fall, I shall arise; when I sit in darkness, the LORD shall be a light unto me" (Micah 7:8). Sweeter words were never spoken to someone who has been put on the shelf and is waiting on the good hand of the Lord to bring them out to the light of day again. And all the time you were thinking that you were holding onto His hand, actually He was holding yours, because you might have turned loose at the wrong moment and because He loves you more than you'll ever know in this life.

CHAPTER 6

Seeking an invisible God is often harder to accomplish than to write about. I often prayed for a visible manifestation of God's nearness. I would pray, "Here I am, Lord. I give all my heart to You. Here I am. And it seemed I felt in my heart that God was seeking me. The chorus of a favorite song says, "Let your Spirit move through me. Here I am." In church, we sing a chorus so similar to this that it seems I quoted it, but I think God speaks to us through many ways. We are like newborn infants when it comes to being aware of the presence of God. There is a time of adjustment in which the focusing of the eyes occurs at a specific rate of development. Sometimes I feel that I am able to focus spiritual eyes upon something brand new that I've never been able to see before. And then there are times when I can barely make out the outline or image of what I am looking intently toward. Maybe it has always existed there, and maybe it was just always out of focus of my spiritual vision. When God places us in the darkened environment on a shelf for our education, growth, or spiritual preparation, I believe that our eyes become more sensitive to His presence than usual.

"The LORD is good, a strong hold in the day of trouble; and he knoweth them that trust in him" (Nahum 1:7). We need to pray for a greater sensitivity for God's presence in our ministry and to be aware of His presence during and after the times of testing. When we pray for God's presence to be a part of our ministry and daily lives, we really are asking for a divine manifestation to be our rod and staff to keep us from staggering. We want the everlasting arms of God's strength and mercy beneath us so no matter how low we get, we'll never get beneath God's arms of protection, while above us is the canopy or umbrella of the banner of His love. He prepares a banquet table before us in the presence of those who oppose and hinder our progress, and goodness and mercy follow us all the days of our lives.

Folks, we are surrounded by His Spirit. Seeking Him is not strange for He is all around, all the time. There isn't any need to seek what isn't lost. He promised never to leave or forsake us. It's settled. If you feel lost in the place you find yourself spiritually, are you seeking God's presence for what He does for you? Or are you seeking God's presence for who He is in your life? Beware of an overcoming desire to seek the experience of God's nearness and miss the entire purpose in drawing near to Him. Don't choose goose bumps over God's Word.

My mother handed me a poem one day that started out with these words: "I got up early one morning and rushed right into the day: I had so much to accomplish that I didn't have time to pray." It was ironic, but that was happening to me. My prayer life had been in shambles. Fasting was nonexistent. Bible study was a frantic scrambling on the night before a service. I was slowly losing my grip on what had been a steady-as-a-rock commitment to my duties as pastor and as a Christian. We are Christians first, and pastors second.

What was happening to me? Simply put, I didn't know the value of prayer before the work that had been set before me. My immaturity and ignorance of the uncharted waters of busyness were about to run me aground on the rocks that were hidden beneath the surface of my own self-importance. Psalm 23 reminds us, "Yea though I walk through the valley ..." The valley can be a test, a trial, or trouble. It really isn't so hard to bear, if you remember that it's a walk-through not a sleepover. A valley is referred to in the Bible as a cleft in the mountains. A cleft can be a low place among the hills and usually means along a stream. In the valley, it turns dark quickly when the sun goes down. You have the sensation of being down deep, and claustrophobic. You often travel through the valley to get to the place God wants you to be. I heard about a person in Oklahoma who had just lost everything after a tornado hit her home and destroyed her world. She explained, "I have lost everything, but I've still got my life." She was on the other side of her valley. She came through the troubled place, walking out of it with her life.

It's one thing to go through a devastating experience. It's another to get to the other side and testify about it. After this shelf experience, you will have a testimony like no other. It will be filled with humility, thanksgiving, and profound renewed strength. It will be a restoration point in your life never to be forgotten. It will be a place of refreshing from that point onward. You will be a changed person from the inside out.

There are very few shortcuts to get to where God wants you to be. You have to go through some things to get to where God wants you to be. When you try to take the shortcut, you are prone to miss some lessons that will be beneficial to you down the road. Jesus went up into the mountain apart to pray. He was alone and was apart from all the crowds. You can be in the valley or on a mountaintop, but you'd better know how to pray. Read the Bible. Sing to yourself. Encourage yourself. Listen to good music, and listen to old sermons. Jesus will show you how to live through whatever the world throws at you. Don't run from suffering—embrace it. Take up the cross of Jesus. Follow Him and He will show you how to go through the valley. Patience restores. It takes time to heal brokenness. A broken and contrite spirit is God's habitation. He is nearer to you in the valley than at any other time perhaps. It seemed that way as I looked back over the experiences in my life. My lonely times were the most peaceful and lovely times of refreshing that could be, and I would not trade anything for those days alone with my Lord. There are still days I'd like to be all alone with Christ my Lord, and I could tell Him of my troubles all alone. The potter's shelf can sometimes be a place of suffering for you. At times, it has been for me. I remember it well.

When the Master Potter lovingly places you on His shelf of waiting and covers that lump of moist clay with the old, damp burlap for who knows how long, it can become wearisome and a lonely feeling of leaving behind all you have lived for. But something changes, and God's strategy for you begins to take shape; you begin to yield where once you resisted. I've been on the mountaintops and in valleys. I like the mountaintops. But I like to eat, so unless I brought a sack lunch, I have to descend to the valley where the food is found. There will be mountaintops of emotions and valleys of depression, but prayer is the equalizer that brings understanding between the two spheres. Prayer balances the view of the journey of your change from one level to the next in God's kingdom. Mountaintops are for seeing, and valleys are for traveling. People usually want to see where they want to go. They forget that the journey of a thousand miles begins with that first step. God is nearer to you in the valley than at any other time of your ministry. It seemed that way to me at one point in my life. Days turned into weeks, faithfully falling on my knees at the altar of submission became months, and I finally found the doors of opportunity opening just a small crack. It was a welcomed relief.

Many are going through something that threatens to destroy all hope of rescue. The promise of Jesus is if we lose ourselves in His work and follow and serve Him, He will show us how to get through it. And the way He shows me how to get through it may not be the way He'll show you. Sitting on the shelf in the potter's house can be miserable, or it can be peaceful. It can be turmoil, or it can be rest. It can be upheaval, or it can be restoration. Eventually, if you hold on and stay faithful, you will come out of the fog and realize you have been going someplace after all. The race is not to the fast and fancy but to the plodders. Even the plodders get to dance victory's dance. You will arrive one day at the destiny of God's choosing. He charted your steps a long time ago. You will see why He prepared you so carefully on the shelf. When you look back down that road and know the whys, it will be worth it all.

One of the things I've learned is that God's grace and mercy have gotten me through every turn, every snare. I searched for Him, sought for His manifestation, and really thought God was not in the places where I thought He would have been. In the moments and places where I thought God would be absent, I am a witness that He showed up. And whatever burdens you're bearing now or you're about to bear, or trials you are about to go through, His strength and power, grace and mercy, and love will be sufficient. In his footsteps, you will walk every day.

When the storm clouds rise in your life, when disaster, sickness, and death follow you, don't fight it. Jesus said, "Embrace it," and He will show you how to walk through the middle of it without harm. Embracing disaster, sickness, or death is not done very easily. It must be fought for and conquered. Turn loose of your preconceived concepts and pick up your cross. That is where Jesus will be. God does work in ways that are mysterious. We ought to stop telling God the way to bless us; we ought to stop telling God what the other side is supposed to look like, because God knows what we are going through. God has prepared a brighter day and a better way. God has already opened the door and made a new experience for you to enjoy. Don't give up, don't throw in the towel, don't hang it up, and don't stop until you get to victory.

Being on the shelf can be exciting sometimes. Endure to the end, and there is a crown of righteousness. Whatever you are going through, there's nothing too big or too small to take to God. If it's your season to go through it, go through it. If you're not going through something now, you may have been spared. But know this: Your season is coming, and you will go through something one day. Whenever or whatever you go through, you can be victorious. You will have to travel the valley to get through the valley, because sitting on the shelf in the potter's house is not a permanent position.

I am telling you, "Go forward." Even if the brook dries up, there is a place called the crucible. A place of the heat. The hot furnace of trial. But even there, God will take care of you.

CHAPTER 7

The finished product is not ready for the wheel, until He is ready. When He is ready, it will go into the heat of the oven and bake. The feeling of moving forward is so strong now. I get the sense that I'm almost a finished product and I'm ready to go back to work in the vineyard. I can feel it. It's this close. He's still working on me to make me what I ought to be, and the finished product is not like anything anyone has ever seen. As he holds me in his hands, turning me this way and that way to look at this new creation, realizing His dreams, the Lord must look at us all somewhat in the same way. When we get close to the place He's designed for us, the excitement must build in His heart. How He wants us to turn out just as He designed. His expectation level rises as we take on the form and characteristics He envisioned and planned for each of us. These changes bring Him much joy as He anticipates a harvest from the investment He has made in our lives.

I enjoyed the pottery classes in our school's art studio. I was introduced to a small, rectangular block of gray clay. It was nothing but clay at this point: cold, hard, and wrapped in plastic. Our teacher encouraged us to look at the lump of plastic wrapped clay and imagine what was hidden within it. I looked and looked, but I couldn't see anything but shapeless clay. She began to show us pieces of pottery that she had formed and showed us that what was before us on our desks could be transformed into whatever we wanted it to be. Unwrapping the clay and proceeding to become acquainted with my potential treasure was like meeting a person for the first time. It was cold, stiff, unresponsive, and lifeless, but at least it was a beginning. I had to squeeze the clay that was resisting my attempts to get to know it. It was hard, so I added pressure. At first it was unresponsive, and until I warmed it up with much massaging, it seemed unmanageable. With a lot of effort, I got it rolled into a ball. Standing up beside my desk to get more leverage, I slammed my fist down into the ball of clay, flattening it out. Working this way for about an hour, rolling, flattening, rolling, and flattening, I got all of the air and impurities worked out of the clay before I began to create what I envisioned it could become. It was a hard process. I had never worked with clay before, and as the art class ended, I covered the unfinished clay with a moist towel and then placed it on a shelf in a dark, cool closet. There it sat, ready and waiting for the next session.

As a budding potter, I would be required to decide what shape and usefulness my lump of clay would obtain. Would it be a useful work of art, or would it just be an ugly attempt at humor? One day can be a long time, especially for the clay, and a lot of things can happen between getting the clay ready for molding and actually placing it into use as a finished object. The day came when I took my clay out of the dark closet, set it on the table, pressed it once more to check for impurities I might have overlooked, and again began squeezing, flattening, and rolling it into shape. I scooped my clay up, approached the spinning potter's wheel, poised over the center of the wheel, and threw the clay onto the spinning wheel. Around and around it turned. Moistening my hands with water, I put my hands on the clay and began to press gently. Shaping the clay into the object my imagination was directing took a lot of concentration. I was the creator of what I had envisioned. As it rose up from the surface of the wheel, I pressed my thumbs down into the center and, using my thumb and finger, gave it a ribbed design. Was it a vase, was it a bowl, or was it an odd object d'art spinning before me? Stopping the spinning wheel and taking a thin wire, I separated the clay from the wheel, gently lifted it up, and carried it to a drying area. It dried by evaporation those first few hours. Later, I would decorate, paint, and glaze the new pottery, before placing it into the kiln to bake. When the oven automatically shut off and we returned to open the oven door, my heart was in my throat. I used asbestos gloves to pick up my creation. Nervously placing the clay vase on my table, I sat looking at it from all sides. Like a proud papa seeing his firstborn child, I was grinning and thinking, *I made that. That's my creation, and it's beautiful.* It was a part of my imagination. What I first saw in that lump of gray, cold clay at the start was lifeless, but now it had life, color, and a potential use.

Being on that shelf hasn't been all that bad after all, for all things were changed when He found me. A new day broke through all around me, and then I met the Potter. Now I walk no more in the night. There will be a use for every clay that remains pliable and patient. The stiff and unyielding clay will be thrown out into the field castoffs, and that doesn't sound like a very desirable place to be.

When the Master Potter collects you for His chosen selection, you will emerge as a useful product in the place that He puts you. As I sit writing, I'm looking out of my window at a group of eight-, nine-, and ten-year-olds playing softball. Some are more skillful than others. Some don't even know if a softball is really soft, but all I see are lumps of clay that will one day be molded into something useful. Pressed, squeezed, shaped, and placed in the oven of life, wondering what they will become, while the Master looks on as He envisions their future. I wonder what the short one in the orange T-shirt with the blue jeans and blue ball cap will be in just ten short years? Will he be a high school dropout? A drug addict? A teenage father? Will he, with the process that God has planned for him, become a Sunday school teacher? Or begin his first semester of college?

You can't tell just by looking at a lump of clay what the potter intends for it, unless you're the potter. The clay doesn't speak to the potter. It's the mind of the potter being formed through his hands that reveals his plans. You may not be enjoying your time in the dark closet on the shelf, but if you're that far along, then the next process has to be out of the darkness and into His astonishing light. Don't fret. I felt like I would die in there before I felt any moving or direction at all. I didn't have a church to pastor, and there were no sermons to prepare for the midweek meeting or Sunday services. I attended church faithfully, but I felt like a fish out of water each time I sat in those pews. I was sure my destiny was behind a pulpit, but you can't force God's hand. Each and every day was a disappointing conclusion to the fact that I was just on the shelf. My prayer many times was "Lord, let today be the day that You open the door of my ministry and opportunities for new things for me." Here I was, on the sidelines of action, while my friends and fellow pastors reported the glorious news of what was going on in their services. I only wanted to get out of this holding pattern and get back into the harness of pastoring or at least preaching. But there was no change. Finally my tune was "Just let something good happen to me today," and eventually I submitted it all and said, "Not my will, not my will."

Working each day was at least a distraction from the pressure I felt to be about my Father's business. When the morning breaks interrupted my workday, I would walk out of the office and onto the surrounding park where there was a small garden. On a bench facing the park, I would drink my coffee and pray silently. Sometimes a groan would slip out, and I'd look around nervously to see if anyone heard me. I wanted to get on with the business of God's work. God was working all the time to get me ready to do a particular job that I was not quite ready to assume. One year went by, then two, and I continued to pray and study my Bible. On occasion, my pastor would invite me to preach and stretch my wings. Filling in for him in his absence was a blessing. During these times, it felt good to be useful and not to be idle. It was part of the potter's plan of gently applying pressure to the right spots of the clay to produce the desired vessel.

Are you waiting on God to finish the work He has begun in your heart? He will not forsake you. You are not alone. There are hundreds of men and women not unlike you who are waiting patiently for God to finish the work He started in them. Our Bible says "he is able to finish the work he has begun in you" (Philippians 1:6). Is just sitting on a pew in somebody's church getting to you? Well, if you ever expect to get to where you think you're supposed to be going, you'd better just sit for a while longer. At least until you feel the hand of the Master moving you.

One day I began to feel that God was about to use me again. I got excited and shared this news with my wife. I said, "I feel like God is about to put me back in the saddle." She looked at me with that knowing glance and replied, "Uh huh. What else is new?" Turning back to the sink of dishes, she wondered aloud, "And just when is this feeling of yours going to become something that you are definite about?" I mumbled, "I'm not sure when, but it's so close." As I rubbed the tip of my index finger and thumb together in a rolling manner, I said, "It's this close. I know it is." She replied with all of the faith of a shelved preacher's wife, "I'll believe it when I see it." She didn't feel as positive as I did at the moment, but she was a great sounding board.

Now I knew that was not what faith was made of, but what was I to do? How could I get her to join with my faith? I couldn't. Not this time. It was a one-man "claymanship." God would continue to work with me for six more months. During these months, I fasted and prayed more for direction. I began to study the Bible like it was the map to a buried treasure, and it was. I would get up at 3:00 a.m., go into the living room, bury my face in my hands, kneel at my chair, break through the sleepiness, and submit fully. It was the decorating of my vessel.

I look back fondly now, but it was torture.

Today, I'm grateful that God didn't listen to my ignorant ravings about me knowing where an empty pulpit was. He was working on me. To make me what He wanted me to become. One morning, it was different. Different to me in that the scriptures I was reading spoke to me with a clarity that caused me to catch my breath. There was a group somewhere crying out for a shepherd to lead them. Somewhere, doors were opening. Laying my Bible down and lifting my hands toward heaven, I prayed, "Oh God, lead me to these people. Show me where to go, if You're ready for me to go." Whether I heard it audibly or just in my heart, my heart leaped at the feeling I got. My wife had joined me in prayer by this time and I shared with her what God had impressed on me. She began to read from her Bible, and it literally caused me to shout—quietly, for it was still early and the kids weren't up for school yet. And her scriptures confirmed what I had been impressed to read.

I didn't know how fast God was going to get me ready to get off the shelf. After a Sunday night service, a visiting evangelist introduced himself to me and we began talking about my background in the ministry, his evangelistic travels, and so forth. Then he said, "Did you know that a certain church was searching for a pastor?" I told him, "Where in the world is that located?" He told me what city it was near and all the who, what, where, and when. With a handshake, we parted ways.

On the forty-five-minute drive home, I repeated the brief conversation to my wife. She said, "Well, why don't you call. What can it hurt?" I was nervous. "Me. That's who it can hurt. I don't want to be on the shelf longer because I was impatient." She insisted. "You call when we get home." So I did.

The man in charge was a wise, elderly gentleman who had spent years in the ministry and knew the voice of the Lord. He quickly told me the story. It didn't look too good to get a chance to interview, but he would mention my name before they closed the hearing for potential pastors. My wife said, "Well, we might get a chance."

The following Wednesday morning, the elderly man in charge of this church called me. He said, "Brother, I told the church of your interest, and they'd like to hear you preach this Sunday." We did. And then I was elected as pastor. I was off the shelf and in the pulpit. God blessed us mightily. I have learned that you must not force God's timetable. I have been tempted so many times to make it happen, but I am so very glad that I have waited on God to open the doors.

God knows where you are. God knows your address. And God knows how to get in touch with you. But you know what? I believe that the Lord "made as if he would pass me by." I asked Him to come in. He responded, and the rest is history.

Or is it?

I still feel the effects of His mighty arms around me. Often, I can feel the pressure of His desires, and the marks are still fresh in my heart. There was a time when I didn't think anyone cared for my soul, not even God. But God did. He cared. He loves me, and He loves you too. Don't listen to all the negative speech and the false words of the enemy. The battle is often between your ears, not with another person. Believe the truth. Generate good thoughts and positive statements, open your mouth, and God will fill it with the words of victory. Only Jesus can satisfy your soul with hopes and dreams that can be fulfilled.

One day, I was talking with a fellow minister who happened to be between pastoral positions. He was getting frustrated with the church interview procedures. I couldn't help but see myself as he was telling me about the heartaches, the disappointments, the late-night crying sessions, the pity parties, and the anger and resentment he struggled with. "You are on target, my brother," I said. "You are right where

God wants you." He looked at me like I had just fallen off of a turnip wagon. "That's right. God is working on your behalf, and you just don't recognize it yet." He said, "Oh, I know God is going to take care of us. It's just the waiting and waiting and waiting some more that's wearing me down." "Yes, that is a bit tiring, but when you're on the shelf, you wait until God has a special need for your abilities, your skills, and your attitude." "On the shelf?" he asked. And I began to tell him about the steps of progress I have taken on this journey of growth. I told him about the sermon I heard one day on the potter's house found in the book of Jeremiah and the statement the pastor made about the shelf where the potter kept the clay that he was continuing to work with. That shelf was where I was, and that shelf was where he was.

You can call it what you want to, but for me and many others, it's a shelf of sitting down and gritting your teeth, waiting until you think you will dry up and blow away or wither and become hard and set. Your time of effectiveness passes by and the victory will pass, and you feel like you will pass away. *What's the use?* you think. You can be on the shelf, yet you must be ready to move. When the Holy Spirit opens the door for you, be ready to move. Remain pliable, useable, teachable, and yielded to the impression God is pressing and molding into your life. Beware of bitterness. It may be a hard pill to swallow, but bitterness may be the deadliest enemy of all. The hurt, offended feelings produce the bitter gall of vengeful thoughts that will wreck your chances of becoming just what God wants to produce through you. Guard yourself with a sweet and humble attitude.

So many ministers get weary in waiting on God to mature their ministries and miss the golden opportunity to be crafted into the exact vessel of God's desire for the right time and the right place with the right people. God will match the man with the job. When you need a drink of water, you don't get a swimming pool to drink out of; just a glass will do. Or if you need a boiler to boil an egg in, you wouldn't get a number three washtub to cook it in. Nor will your heavenly Father put you in a place you'd be mismatched for. You can't use a block of clay to put food or drink in, and God can't use a preacher who's not ready to be used. He is headed for shelf time.

No matter how great you think you are, God sees through your visions of grandeur and sees possibilities you can be but don't yet possess the capability for. Don't despise the day of small things. Every great ministry, church, or organization has in its history a very small beginning. Ideas are just figments of our imaginations until they become thoughts in action, and then they become realities. *On the shelf* was God's proving ground for me. These words have helped me understand my destiny as a towel bearer like Jesus. He took a towel and washed the feet of His disciples. We are just servants. Anything more and we might get out of place.

CHAPTER 8

How May I Serve You?

He didn't come as a King, nor did He a sword or scepter bring, but as a Servant, with His towel held ready, to give freely, what men could not buy, His love, for all eternity. And so I come, not as the vicar of Christ, not as reverend, but as a servant with the towel draped over my arm saying, "How may I serve you, my friends?"
—James E. Brooks

Traveling from state to state and church to church provided me with an opportunity to receive firsthand the experiences of being sidelined on the shelf until God opened the door of opportunity for my particular ministry. Many days of fasting and prayer passed by without an answer from heaven, but I knew to stay on my knees until it did come. So many just give up after the first big disappointment sets in and never give the timing of God another chance to operate. God does have a plan for you, but you must learn to wait upon it.

In every shift of my own ministry, I learned to wait on direction and open doors. I now know that a closed door is a good thing when you have submitted your life to the Lord's hands. The closed door simply means that an open door means to go forward. We then pray for wisdom to take that step of faith to move into the realm of the supernatural possibility of new things.

Never doubt, never look back, but always go forward in faith. Being on the shelf allows the opportunity to strengthen the prayer life. Many will pray and ask for guidance in making decisions and then wonder how they will know what God's answer is when a choice must be made. The open-door prayer system that I believe in and use teaches that when God has put you on the shelf of waiting for a period of undisclosed time, you must ask God to close all the doors that will lead the wrong way and to open all the doors which He would have you take. This takes a strong faith because you must believe that every closed door is God's answer and not a rejection of any kind.

Promise to go forward through the open door with courage and faith and that the open door has been opened for you by Him. Be sure this is what He would have you do. God moves in mysterious ways, and often we become impatient for doors to open, but we must have faith and wait. God will guide you down life's paths, and He will keep His promise made in Jeremiah 33:3. "Call unto me, and I will answer thee, and shew thee great and mighty things which thou knowest not."

Can you believe that the shelf is a place of safety and sanctuary, a place where your values are reexamined and carefully prioritized? It is an incubator for men and women God wants to use. It is a place where the rough is smoothed down and the sharp is softened. You can't be a bulldozer for Christ and polish fine china at the same time. And you can't move mountains with a teaspoon collection either. God needs the sledgehammer ministry and the jeweler's hammer ministry. Sometimes He needs the power of a jackhammer. "Is not my word like as a fire? Saith the LORD; and like a hammer that breaketh the rock in pieces?" (Jeremiah 23:29 KJV). And sometimes He needs the gentle finesse of a surgeon's skill. You see people are His main concern. He came to seek and to save that which is lost. So He made the choice to use the foolishness of preaching to reach out to the unguided masses of humanity.

God uses the flesh to reach out to the flesh of mankind. He has chosen you and me. He has chosen others. He teaches us, trains us, develops us, and educates us to be soul winners and witnesses of His kingdom. We are created in His image, of course, so each vessel He has created will have the crest of the King imprinted on it somewhere. Understand that God will not use foolish men to do a holy work but men who've been honed to a razor's edge of service to use the foolishness of preaching to reach the lost and encourage the church. Men and women who have humbled themselves in the sight of the Lord and have prayed these words:

> Oh that thou wouldest bless me indeed, and enlarge my coast, and that thine hand might be with me, and that thou wouldest keep me from evil, that it may not grieve me. And God granted him that which he requested. (1 Chronicles 4:10)

It sounds to me like Jabez may have sat on the shelf in the potter's house somewhere. Until God got ready to move him, use him and bless him, God didn't lift a finger for old Jabez. God doesn't tune up his ministers to make racers out of them. No, He makes His ministers to be flames of fire. You can be a racer or a keeper of the flame. I simply want to be what He wants me to be. We don't want to be Roman candle Christians, to flame across the sky and just burn out. We need to be steady lights in the night of darkness. No more, no less. You are going to be presented with opportunities to be more for the Lord, but the Lord will pass you right on by unless you constrain Him to abide with you. Stay in His presence when the flames of adversity leap up around you, stay in His presence when you can't see in the darkness, and stay in His presence when you have lost all sense of direction. For in His presence, you will find fullness of joy, peace, vision, and direction.

If you feel like a failure, then let me tell you about my Friend. He specializes in picking up the broken pieces of your life and reconstructing them in such a fashion that you're better made when He pronounces you cured. The man who cannot be master of a small place will never be master in any place. He who does not wish to do more than he can usually winds up by doing less than he should. "He who plows not in his closet, will never reap in his pulpit" (Charles Spurgeon). Do what you have to do and *then do more*. The then more men make the most powerful contributions to their ministerial callings.

"Well done, thou good and faithful servant" is a statement that really says it all. Seven words that will be worth it all when you see Jesus Christ. It covers a lot of range when you apply it to that shelf you've been left on. We must work for the Lord, whenever and wherever the work to be done is found, and we must begin now.

I received a phone call from a friend with a message that was very encouraging. He told me that he saw me holding a beautiful cup that was encrusted with jewels and precious stones of every description. But it was empty. It was a cup that was the envy of many who saw its luster and glow. As he watched, the light of this wonderful cup dimmed, the cup aged, the stones disappeared, and the glow was extinguished. The once beautiful cup was replaced with an aged-looking, dented, and well-used cup that nobody would have given a second glance to. But now this cup was filled to the brim. Filled with what everyone wanted.

Could he have seen the life of a minister before he experiences the shelf experience as that beautiful cup of jewels? The dull, simple cup seems to fit perfectly with the Master's desire as useful. This is what I found after giving myself to faithful prayer and yielding humbly to the Master and to His will. Was the before and after of these cups the difference in giving myself to solitude and becoming sensitive to the voice that speaks so softly and lowly and the abandoning of the carefree life of prideful selfishness?

A broken and contrite spirit is what the Lord desired in my life. Give the Lord what He calls for, and receive everything you desired. May you find the prize and win the victory that God wants so much to give you. Stay on the shelf until the Master Potter is ready for you to go where He decides.

Patience, my friend.

Printed in the United States
By Bookmasters